WHY AM I?

WHY AM I?

FIND THE MEANING OF LIFE • LIVE WITH
PURPOSE • SUCCEED ON YOUR TERMS

TODD WHITAKER

ODDWARD BOOKS

Published by Oddward Books

Las Vegas, Nevada

Library of Congress Cataloging-in-Publication Data

Whitaker, T. E.

Why Am I? / T. E. Whitaker

p. cm.

ISBN 978-0-9914798-0-1

eBook ISBN 978-0-9914798-1-8

1. Self-Help—General2. Philosophy—Non-fiction

Library of Congress Control Number: 2014901358

First Edition 2014

Book design by Viola Wyatt

10 9 8 7 6 5 4 3 2 1

CONTENTS

ACKNOWLEDGMENTS

My thanks to everyone who, knowingly or not, contributed an ear or a thought to my philosophy of meaning, purpose, and fulfillment. First, there's my brother, who provided the needed shove toward doing something with all the thoughts swimming in my head, as detailed in this book's prologue. Then there are my parents who, since my birth, have walked the razor's edge between normal conversation and my monological tendencies. Their bravery in the face of such a verbose child cannot be overstated. Thanks, Mom and Dad. Though there is a significant list of friends who, at one time or another, have found themselves on the business end of one of my half-baked ideas, I would like to specifically thank Dean, Elaine, Eugene, and Mike for our countless conversations, struggles, and adventures over the years, many of which have helped shape the thoughts expressed in this book. Finally, thank you to my family—Viola, Wyatt, and Mischa—for their patience and love.

INTRODUCTION

I waited for my brother to answer the question. After twenty years in Los Angeles, I'd moved back home for family and financial reasons. Now, four months into my "living in the Midwest as an adult" experiment, my kids seemed happier, and because of the dramatic cost-of-living decrease, my financial issues had dissolved. Still, a deeper problem had made the move with me, and I'd recently recognized my failure to escape the hard-charging panic I'd experienced in my last months in California. Despite my wonderful family, I still felt deeply unhappy and unfulfilled.

Was I experiencing an existential crisis?

A third reason I'd moved back home was to reconnect with my brother. We were close, but despite semi-regular phone calls, I felt we'd drifted apart over the past few years. He was the person who knew me best in the world, and I wanted to regain that closeness. I hoped he would give me an unvarnished answer.

My question was, "What's wrong with me?"

I'm not insecure. If anything, I'm optimistic regarding my abilities and intellect, but despite what I considered my best efforts—an asser-
my father would argue—life had not worked out as fabulously as

I'd expected. I'd played college baseball, but not pro. I'd moved to Los Angeles to be a film director but, instead of pursuing a career in film, had written a series of unpublished novels. Full disclosure: I had directed two short films and a feature-length film, but they were small, for the most part unseen except in a couple of festivals, and hadn't brought me the riches and worldwide adulation I'd hoped for. To pay for semi-pursuing a film career and completely pursuing the L.A. lifestyle of clubbing and al fresco dining, I'd held multiple jobs in multiple companies, all marketing-related, and never committed to any of them. A stint as a fitness business owner and trainer had proved runaway successful on multiple levels before declining because of personal issues and my waning interest. Nothing ever seemed to work out.

The above paragraph is essentially what I recounted to my brother before asking (despite the warnings of every success expert and guru who ever suggested, stressed, or screamed to rephrase every question in the positive), "What's wrong with me?"

Negative questions do not always lead to positive answers, but I've become convinced that, because of the forces at work in today's world, it's necessary to determine and understand what's wrong with life as you know it *before* you can fix it.

If you've had life experiences similar to my own—meaning you're alive in this world and you've dated and/or married and you've held jobs, all the usual things—there is no doubt negative questions have value. When your romantic relationships haven't worked out as you may have wished, or you've somehow failed at jobs that didn't challenge you, eventually you have to notice the common factor in your failings is you. This was the first—and maybe the most important—epiphany I had:

I was the problem.

It came to me a few microseconds before I decided to drop by my brother's office for a straightforward chat. Somewhere along the road I'd become my enemy, but I didn't know where or when.

My hunch was that taking responsibility for the negatives in my own sand, your own stick, and to stand with you while you draw your line.

To Be Who You Truly Are, First You Must Think

Determining the meaning and purpose of your life is a process. Though the answers will vary for everyone, the process itself is essentially the same. *Why Am I?* begins with thoughts on why the evolution of our ideas, beliefs, and values has left most of us with a lost, wanting feeling. I'll offer insight as to why even the most successful among us (by society's standards) are no closer to fulfillment—and sometimes further away—than anyone else. Shouldn't the attainment of economic goals equal happiness and fulfillment? That's what we're told, and that's what we're sold. But it doesn't. Material acquisition is like eating. No matter how much you eat, no matter how full you are for the moment, inevitably you will be hungry again.

My purpose in writing this book is to put an end to this kind of hunger, the hunger that eats at you when things are dark and quiet, when your inner voice asks the uncomfortable questions about what you're doing with your life. My purpose is to offer you a specific, realistic path to fulfillment, to help you consciously ask the uncomfortable questions so you can answer them, take action on those answers, and live a continually fulfilling life.

I'm a practical philosopher, not a guru. I'm not going to give you half-baked, serpentine pronouncements on the nature of life and a parallel, unseen world. I won't tell you the answer to everything is to "just love." This sort of advice, the sort that provides nothing more than a quick endorphin rush to the soul and a few days of feel good, won't get you any closer to meaningful fulfillment in the real world, the world where you must live and function and pay real money for products and services.

Why Am I? is for you if you'd like to fill your days with deep meaning, purpose, and fulfillment while living in the real world.

I'll identify the major elements and standards of today's world preventing you from reaching fulfillment. I'll provide the necessary questions to help you determine the unique meaning of your life as well as a process to translate your meaning into your purpose. I'll ask the questions, and you'll provide the answers. Be honest with yourself, and you'll emerge from *Why Am I?* with the meaning and purpose of existence—*your* existence.

Why Am I? provides questions, space to write your answers, and notes when I think it might help. That said, I'll take care while guiding you through the process. The major hurdle between you and your fulfillment is the army of external influences vying for your attention, your agreement, and your resignation, every day from birth to death. I refuse to add my voice to the cacophony. The only voice that matters is yours.

To get the most out of *Why Am I?* and emerge with a clear purpose, read the book and perform the exercises in order. Lifelong fulfillment depends on how you live, which is guided by your purpose, which is based on the unique meaning of your life. Skipping around is a surefire way to cheat yourself of the experience and to minimize the epiphanies, clarity, and sudden understandings that come with deep consideration and honest internal dialogue. You've lived this long unfulfilled. There is simultaneously no hurry and a desperate urgency.

With that in mind, let's begin.

TODD WHITAKER
September 2013

life and pinning them squarely on myself might enable me to solve problems that had plagued me every step of my adult life in relationships, jobs, sports—in *everything*.

I accepted that I was the problem. I knew it going in. What I didn't understand was *why*, and what I wouldn't understand for some time was the two-sided-coin nature of my brother's answer. It would be even longer before I grasped that this dual realization presented an explanation, a riddle, and an elegant solution.

I waited. He watched me, his fingers forming a steeple, a thinking gesture we share. I guessed he was deciding how straightforward he wanted to be.

"Well?"

He sat back in his chair and said, "You're uncoachable."

Be aware, as you're reading about the moments leading to my epiphany, that this was far from the first time I'd heard this sort of thing, usually in the company of phrases such as *untapped potential* and *arrogant*. I'd always brushed off criticism like this by silently questioning the evaluator's motivations.

My brother had no ulterior motive. There was nothing in it for him either way, not in the usual, culturally agreed-upon measures of profit. My self-discovery wouldn't lead him to greater financial gain. It wouldn't give him higher social standing.

"You think you don't need anyone else," he said. "You don't play the game. You don't even try to get along."

I began to speak, but he cut me off. "Everything was easy for you early on, and I think you expected it to always be that way, so you've avoided things that might challenge your high opinion of yourself."

I was pacing back and forth across his office. I'd committed to listening before I'd asked my question regardless of where it led, no matter what he said, or how much it stung. Still, the urge to lash back with perfectly logical, unassailable reasoning as to why he was wrong —apparently, a well-known strategy of mine—threatened to overwhelm my commitment. He was pissing me off, but he was right, and my brother can argue both sides of an issue better than I can. It wasn't a battle I could win.

"You're not like anyone else," he continued, taking the edge off, at least for the moment. "And that's fine and maybe even good, but you don't capitalize on your talents. You don't stretch them. You don't share anything. You have all these ideas and theories, but you don't put them out there. You bitch about things, but you never do anything about it."

Again, he had nailed it. Was I writing anything? No. Was I working on anything of any value whatsoever? No. I was a coffee shop philosopher destined to die with an over-honeyed espresso in my hand, without finishing anything or helping anyone or contributing anything to the world.

"Okay," I said, stopping at the corner of his desk. "What should I do?"

"How should I know?" he said. "Do something good, something that isn't easy for you. Create something valuable. Take a stand."

His words "take a stand" hit me gut deep. Like most people, I'd always hoped—if a situation demanded it—I'd be brave, but I'd always assumed it would be physical bravery.

I hadn't considered bravery or taking a stand as a life choice.

There are two songs I listen to frequently: Emili Sandé's "Read All About It, Pt. III" and Bon Jovi's "It's My Life." Though their styles contrast, the songs put forward similar messages of not being afraid, of standing your ground. Both songs still bring the emotions after countless listens. What is it about bravery, or the idea of taking a stand, that moves me, that moves all of us? Why had I never tried to reconcile how I lived with what I thought, what I valued, and who I really was? What was I waiting for?

Did I even know who I really was?

This book is the result of my search for something to stand for, the quest of a lifelong underachiever to move beyond my café table, to find a place in the sand to draw my line, to pick a fight with what I think is humanity's most crippling problem, to help you find your

PART
ONE

PART ONE
WHY AREN'T I?

Before you can look inside, it's important to understand the external forces working against you every day, steering you toward the many false gods of fulfillment. Among these are religion and spirituality, the expectations of your family and friends, and the material standards set by the media and the world's marketing machines.

THE FIRST QUESTION

Before You Ask, Why Am I? You Have to Ask Yourself, Why Aren't I?

THERE ARE many quotes out there regarding a teacher appearing when the student is ready. With few, if any, exceptions, this refers to a guru of sorts guiding the initiate down the path to enlightenment. Fortunately, it's wrong. You don't need a guru. The truth of the matter is that you are the student, and when you're ready, the teacher —also you—will appear. Like any genuine dialogue or successful investigation, finding your meaning, translating that into purpose, and then living your purpose so you experience fulfillment every day requires the right questions and honest answers—answers that can come only from you. As mentioned in the prologue, I'm going to provide an effective series of questions. Your answers will make the difference in your life.

It's an exciting proposition. You are in control. You determine your course. For possibly the first time, you will determine a deep personal meaning to your life, put action to it to create purpose, live it every day, and experience consistent fulfillment. The fulfillment isn't based on achieving financial independence, mastering internet marketing, placing ads, "creating abundance," turning your life into a series of extended vacations, or attempting other actions you may or may not be able or want to achieve. If you can read and think for yourself, consider questions, and answer them honestly until you've drilled down to what you're really about, what moves you to joy or anger, that infinitely dense singularity within you that makes you *you*, then you can do this. There's nothing to buy or sell. Your only obstacle is you.

But first, you have to put down the story.

Wait. What? What story?

You may be unaware you've been reading a story every day of your life until now—the story of your culture and its externally derived values and beliefs and goals, the story designed to keep you plodding along the beaten path, contributing to a machine over which you exert zero control and to which you make next-to-zero meaningful contribution. It's not because you can't contribute. You *can*, but we're all too wrapped up in striving for or maintaining external standards established long ago, ingrained in each of us by our parents, grandparents, and great-grandparents—the internal tattoos of a modern tribe.

The American Dream—now twisted and bloated beyond recognition and exported throughout the world—has become the economic version of original sin.

The story you've been forced to read—by your family, friends, the media, the marketers, the retailers, and religion—is the story with which we all grow up. It's a churning amalgam of material success pursuits, eternal salvation, hellfire, celebrity worship, lifestyle envy, salving bromides, wedding days, dismaying divorce, apocalyptic distraction, fear-based economics, and age-old wisdom about embracing life's simple things (meant to stem the rising panic inside). It's a story designed to get you from self-consciousness to the grave without making waves in whatever culture you're born into, to be sure you propagate the species (to the tune of 2.1+ children per female), contribute to the economy, and maintain the proper level of civilization, with the promise of life after death, so long as you meekly follow the rules.

So you follow the path and hold yourself to accepted, external standards that cruelly offer little chance of real fulfillment. In your reptilian core, you know it's unlikely you'll ever soar to the material heights where happiness supposedly awaits, gain the celebrity you're told is so important to pursue, achieve enlightenment and eternal youth through hyper-intense exercise, or receive a supernatural reward while you're alive or dead.

Sound familiar?

To me, our story seems like an evil form of cynicism. You're born. You live. You procreate. You hope to live forever after you die. This can't be it, right? *Right?* Why aren't we living meaningfully *while we're alive?*

I ask you, I beg you, to put down your culture's story and look around. Ask yourself how it's going. Could you *ever* have enough money to buy everything ever made? How long does that new car smell fill the void religion and alcohol and marriage and parenthood can't manage? Ask yourself if you're as happy as you want to be. Would a successful blog with a healthy comment section and 15,106 all-powerful "Likes" nurture every fiber of your being? Ask yourself what the hell you're doing with your life. Why are you unthinkingly pursuing what you're told is important? Why do you accept it? What are you teaching your children? If you're active on social media but avoid texting while driving, watch enriching television while keeping up with current events, contribute to the latest internet memes, smile at babies, and by external standards are "successful," why do you feel unfulfilled?

Let me answer this right now. You feel unfulfilled because you've tried to find your meaning and purpose outside yourself. You've looked for it under rocks, in ancient books, between the lines of technical specifications, within the right combination of ingredients, or by hacking your life. You've tried to buy your fulfillment. You've complied with what you're supposed to want, so you've tried materialism and narcissism, but your fourteen-inch pillow top mattress and your new haircut and your clever T-shirt and your interval training didn't do it for you.

You *know* there must be more. There is, but the *more* in life is hidden by the pop culture noise, numbing routine, a fat dose of laziness, and an apparently worldwide unwillingness to think.

What we need is a new story, a new plot, with each of us our own author and architect.

The answers are within you, not without. They're small and elemental. You could not have known them when you were a child because you didn't have the necessary experience or knowledge of the world. Understandably and regardless of age, to this point you've accepted what your parents, teachers, and friends believe, what they value, what they'd learned, *because you are a part of your culture—* like grass in the ground. So be it. Now you owe it to yourself to put an end to it and build the framework for a meaningful, purposeful, fulfilling life.

Can you do it? Of course you can.

The student (you) is ready.

The teacher (you) will now appear.

BEWARE THE IDES OF NOW

Fulfillment Not Guaranteed

WE LIVE in the most dangerous time in history. When I refer to it as dangerous, I don't mean from a terror perspective, and I'm not selling fear. Times *feel* dangerous because of the breathtaking speed of change and the uncertainties inherent within change. But within change is opportunity.

We also live in the most exciting time in history. Never have more tools existed to forge your unique path. But never have more shiny things distracted you from—or prevented you from noticing—your path. The noise around us jerks our attention this way and that.

Countless options surround us, hard facts are disputed, statistics are disfigured. Social media distracts us with frivolity, stress accompanies us on our errands. We're ever more capable of creating and shaping our lives, and ever more at the mercy of forces keen to enslave us within a machine those same forces insist is beneficial, yet benefit those forces alone—if we trust the employment and real wages statistics our corporate and governmental overlords spend millions persuading us aren't real.

We live on the cusp of an employment crisis the likes of which we've never experienced. The tech, healthcare, and service sectors provide the best-paying jobs, but technology companies strive for efficiency, healthcare is in flux, and service businesses require people who can afford services. If wage and income disparity trends continue to accelerate, the lower class will expand, the middle class will contract, and both will weaken.

Though I'm aware some of what I write is politically charged, or sounds like conspiracy crap, I'm not stating anything you didn't now before you cracked this book. The life most politicians, institutions, faceless corporations, and advertisers want you to lead is a life of consumption-based meaning. Do you ever drive to or from work, park, switch off your engine, and wonder "How the hell did I get here?" with the past twenty minutes' turns, lights, traffic, and signs unnoticed and unremembered, a blank portion of your life?

Everyone has. You're not alone.

That twenty minutes' dead zone is your routine, the impermeable membrane of futility and meaninglessness between you and the reality you *could* live. You can't pierce the membrane with time management. You can't do it by blogging. Blogging becomes the membrane, unless blogging about marketing your blog fulfills you with deep, soul-stroking meaning. You can't break the membrane with constant travel, because you are wherever you go.

You pierce the film from within, not from without, by who you are, not what you do. But most of us have never taken the necessary time to determine who we are. And therefore the "same" remains. The grind. The feeling you've lived this day before, a groundhog with opposable thumbs, mechanical inclinations, a too-high car payment, a two-bedroom apartment, and a to-do list you don't do. The urge to do nothing speaks to you, because what you do now, yesterday, tomorrow means nothing.

You know this, you've considered these very things. You've asked yourself what you're going to do with your life, or what you're going to do when you grow up. You and your friends joke about it, you say it as a point of pride at times, as if you're biding your time until you kick it into gear, *it* being your life, which is ticking past as you read these words.

Ergo, this book is blissfully short, so you can get to it, *it* being your *life*.

The Chains of Inertia

If your routine provides for you or you and your family, said routine is comfortable, safe, insulating. There *is* meaning in security, but it's not the meaning we're searching for. We're looking for meaning independent of what you're told to value, independent of trends and time, the meaning buried inside you, resistant to previous half-assed attempts to unearth it, or floating inches below the surface, guarded from discovery by your fear.

The inertia of routine is your enemy. Your enemies are your current habits. Our habits define us, define our lives and what we produce. If you read self-help books about time management, travel blogging, minimalism, and determining the meaning of your life, but don't follow through with the work necessary to manage your time, simplify your spaces, write about traveling, or determine your meaning, you are a reader of self-help books, nothing more.

Execution is everything. To execute is to raze diminishing, stifling, inertial habits in favor of empowering, meaning- and purpose-supporting habits.

Execution is hard. But we live in varying states of disappointment, disillusion, and self-delusion because we don't do the hard things. The hard thing is trading a few days of real self-analysis and consideration *now* for a *lifetime* of fulfillment.

It's difficult. You'll come upon answers you won't like. You'll make discoveries you'd rather had remained buried. Some of your values and ideas on morality may be ugly when exposed to light, but they're you. And without knowing who you really are and what you really value, you will never live a fulfilling life. Happy? Maybe, if you're happy now. Fulfilled? No.

Inertia's chains—lifestyle, stuff, debt, daily stresses, healthcare or lack thereof, tradition, the princess delusion, resistance to change, fear, routine, inability to decide, lack of willpower, self-defeating habits, unnecessary ties—are what stop you from considering your meaning and purpose. They stop us all.

Breaking the chains of inertia requires effort, but no more than waking up every morning and going to a job you hate all day so you can make it to Friday afternoon. I want more for you. *You* want more for you. Commit to yourself. Wield your mental machete and hack through your jungle of routines and bad habits and inertia until you've cut your path.

SELF-INTEREST

The Search for Meaning Can't Be Navigated with GPS

A LOT HAS CHANGED since the first person with the mental capacity to do so peered into the night sky and wondered, *Why am I?*

In the interim between then and now, the question's value has shifted from existential to experiential. At the time, survival was the paramount concern, so the base answer—to survive long enough to make little early humans—was all that mattered. Indeed, one can make a solid argument that the real and only "meaning" of life is to live long enough to procreate, to continue the species—the rock-bottom purpose of all living things. You are here because all of your ancestors were smart enough, fast enough, lucky enough, and survived long enough, to procreate.

But when we ask what the meaning of life is, I don't think any of us are searching for—or are satisfied with—the flat answer "to continue the species." We're searching for what it's all about, what we can do while we're here, how we can make an impact, or maybe how we can not only continue the species but advance it. We're looking for something more, for the experiential answer.

If life is to fulfill, the meaning of life must fulfill.

Unfortunately, the answers we receive from our culture are, at best, momentary misdirection. How long will a new phone feed your hunger to do more with your life? Do you really think an extra bedroom you can use as an office will make it all okay? Will an extra $10,000 spent on your wedding make your subsequent marriage $10,000 stronger? How long will you accept the hope of life after death as a substitute for life now? How long will your parents influence how you live your life? Will you always live in fear? How long will it take for you to realize the best moments of your life happened while you were out there challenging yourself, not while you were sitting in front of the television watching actors live imaginary lives? Doesn't the fact we're all working for vacations and weekends indicate there is something fundamentally wrong with how and why we work?

The search for meaning has moved beyond the biological to, for most, the spiritual or scientific. But spirituality is no more than a socially accepted hallucinogen, and science may not be capable of—and hasn't yet bothered with—defining meaning that resonates. Though many would say the answers lie somewhere between science and spirituality, I think that's a cop-out assertion that sounds good but can't withstand the most surface examination. You've tried them both. So have I. If either did the trick, I wouldn't be writing this book, and you wouldn't be reading it.

Regardless of what side you're on, to figure it all out, you must turn your greatest asset—your mind—inward to answer the questions of existence and meaning.

For the purposes of this book, the "meaning" of life will be what is most important to *you* about yourself and the world at large. Meaning is what you think and value about life based upon your Moral Code, Values Code, and Ideals Code—all of which you'll develop as you move through this book—combined with your reason, experience, and passion.

To discover "Why am I?" first you have to shrug off the story discussed earlier and ignore external influences. You have to ask yourself questions usually considered negative, questions we're erroneously told are unproductive. Speaking from experience, so long as I continued to ask positive questions, altering "What am I doing wrong?" to "How can I do this better?" I was unable to get to the nut of my problems. The hard, simple, liberating truth is that *the problem is always you,* and *the solution is always you.*

You will never find fulfillment by continuing to do what you're doing. If you are unfulfilled, if life has little or no meaning to you, if you're feeling numb or desperate or frustrated, quit making excuses and accept that you're doing it wrong. Ignore the charlatans and the "top ten" lists. A diet won't work. A hobby won't make it all go away. Burying yourself in work will only push you further from the solution.

What's necessary is an examination of your thoughts, beliefs, values, and ideals. Putting yourself under a microscope is the clearest path to finding meaning deep enough and personal enough to fuel your life.

What will you do with it once you've determined the meaning of your life? We're rational beings, but we make gut decisions, decisions we'll never control. How do we clear that hurdle? Are we doomed to peel away the onion with our intellect before helplessly watching our dreams dissolve in tears when our nature kicks in?

It doesn't have to be that way. You *can* put yourself in a place where you'll make your gut decisions within the framework of your life's unique meaning and purpose.

That's part of our strategy. Through the right questions, you'll build your unique framework of meaning and purpose within which to live your life, so the unconscious, gut decisions you make will flow from conscious decisions, informing the actions you take and keeping you on a fulfilling path.

But before we begin building, we must tear down what's already there by exposing the external forces and influences that have subtly and not-so-subtly informed, guided, and/or forced every decision you've made since the day you were born.

MEDIA, MARKETING, AND MATERIALISM

If It's Being Marketed to You, You Probably Don't Need It

ONCE UPON A TIME, happiness without crushing debt was possible. Granted, those halcyon days have dissolved into what most of us view as a worthwhile trade-off: image and toys for credit card debt.

There is a perfect life for sale. We see it every day on magazine covers, in clever commercials, in the emergence of marriage proposal coordinators. It is no longer enough to kneel before the love of your life, extend a gorgeous diamond mined in Sierra Leone's hellholes, and ask for your beloved's hand in marriage. After all, you are a celebrity in your inner circle. You were a first adopter of Audi, well before it supplanted BMW as the suburban car du jour. You are unique and offer an organic, sustainable lifestyle, suitable for social media. For love to truly bloom, your proposal must be planned, coordinated, *perfect*. Otherwise, how can you expect to ramp up the already unrealistic expectations of your lives together?

The perfect life—the life you are told you deserve every time you open your eyes to greet the morning and the promise of a shining, unrelenting marketing onslaught—is always just beyond your means, expanding with each pay raise, receding with every failure, eternally on the horizon, at the end of the rainbow, an infuriatingly elusive pot o' gold.

Chances are you will never reach it no matter how much money you make, no matter how many leprechauns you capture. You cannot buy fulfillment.

We've all heard the phrase "money can't buy happiness," and for the majority of my life I thought that was a load of crap. I certainly behaved and set goals with the clear perspective that accumulation and fulfillment went hand in glove. *Of course* money can buy happiness. But it didn't. Money bought whatever was for sale, and that's an important distinction.

Is happiness for sale?

Is love for sale?

Is fulfillment for sale?

No. These are feelings, internal experiences.

We all know money can't buy anything but what's for sale, and yet we behave as if it can.

We are sold standards of existence the vast majority of us have no chance of attaining. The lifestyles of celebrities and the exceptionally successful are paraded before us as benchmarks of an ideal life. We gobble it up, yearning for a glossy life of excess without questioning whether living such a life will result in happiness.

We are sold fear by the media in every form imaginable, from real dangers to fabricated statistics to outright lies. The world's advertisers, marketers, and pharmaceutical manufacturers sell the accepted cures for fear—stuff that won't contribute to your fulfillment, drugs and outpatient surgeries you don't need, and handguns more likely to kill a family member than a probably-never-gonna-break-in home invader.

Your only chance of conquering fear is attaining financial enlightenment. At least that's what the talking baby on that stock trading commercial told me.

An article on the *New York Times* website, written by Elizabeth

Dunn and Michael Norton, and based on research at Princeton University using Gallup data collected from almost five hundred thousand Americans, indicated that, of course, people are generally happier if they are comfortable as opposed to impoverished. Here are two important points to consider from their article:

- Greater happiness and better moods taper off around $75,000 per year in income. In America, once you earn $75,000 per year, more money will make you no happier
- Although people think their happiness will double if they make twice as much, Dunn and Norton found that people who earn $55,000 per year are only nine percent more satisfied with their lives than those who earn $25,000 per year

Nine percent. Consider that for a moment. That is far less than most credit card interest rates. As a nation, we are incurring soul-crushing debt to attain lifestyle levels that will make us no happier and to buy objects that will do nothing to fulfill us. We are paying 13–22 percent per annum on our debt for a nine percent happiness bump. I realize these numbers aren't statistically comparable, but we can compare them symbolically. Why are we doing it? What is the goal? What do we hope to accomplish?

Why doesn't happiness double when you double your income? I think there is a certain amount of money that buys comfort, and for most people, comfort and contentment are akin to happiness. Once you have a roof over your head, food in the fridge, blankets on the bed, and clothes in the closet, you are comfortable. You are content. You are happy.

Living the Dream

As I'm railing against materialism, I want to be clear about something: I am in no way against having things. I'm not an ascetic. There is no address at the end of this book to which you should send your material possessions. That is not, and will never be, the message I communicate to you. I have likely spent more online time building virtual Porsches than you or anyone you have ever met or mocked. But aside from the undeniable thrill of driving a Porsche, would owning one fulfill me? Would it improve my relationships with others? I love Porsches, and like nearly anyone who loves cars, I can provide a robust list of compelling reasons to drop some serious dosh on one. But I can't say it would make me a more complete person or cause my every step to resound with purpose.

Living your life in lockstep with the messages you receive every day—between songs on the radio, on billboards, in the office, on television, in magazines, and online—will leave all but the most superficial among us empty and all of us in debt.

So why are other people—presumably unfulfilled by materialism themselves—bent on selling us so much meaningless stuff? That's a great question. Is it possible we're sold these things because it's easy to sell objects, but it's difficult to sell meaning and fulfillment? Particularly when you don't need anyone else to find it?

You are the problem. You are the solution.

The barrage will never end. The lifestyle messages building in us an insatiable desire for the material come from not only their purveyors but from their customers, our friends, everyone around us. Every passing moment brings new, creative, invasive methods of reaching the consumer (you and me), making it more difficult to summon an effective defense.

We still wonder why we don't feel happier a few days after purchasing a new phone or why our social lives don't improve incrementally with each step we take toward agreed-upon standards of success. Won't the constant social media reinforcement of our great career, our perfect children, and our clever cat memes bring us the human connection we know we want and need but can't seem to manage because we're so busy?

We post photos of us being fabulous, retweet thoughtful articles about how to organize our lives, grow quietly furious at atrocities in Africa, and photograph every course of every meal we eat, thinking it's the modern equivalent of the close-knit village. We keep up with each other's lives. We're striking a balance between work and home, friends and family. We update. We are updated. We think this is the evolution of friendship, yet whenever we get together with a friend, face to face, for something real like a meal or a party or a baseball game, we find ourselves "catching up" with each other. It seems social media *isn't* so social. It *isn't* an evolution of friendship. It's isolating us together like the yolks inside an egg carton. Now what?

Why are we allowing social media to replace real socializing? Maybe we aren't. Maybe it's a final stand. We feel ourselves slipping away from each other but are unable to resist the internet's pull.

I think social media is a last-ditch effort to prevent our real connections with the world from snapping, but I don't think it will work. All the *likes* and *lols* on earth, all the video chats and texting cannot compete with the most hurried thirty-minute lunch with a good friend.

Well, maybe that beer commercial about squeezing the most out of every day, or the one that tells us life is about "crushing it," contains some deep philosophical truth. Maybe if we crush everything at work, "work hard and play hard," maybe that'll fill the inexplicable emptiness and quiet the gnawing reluctance we feel every Monday morning when the alarm goes off. Maybe we're not *working* hard enough.

So we work harder, play harder, buy more, eat late, sleep less, and pile on the debt, but we succeed only in scratching an itch that won't go away, pushing us to greater levels of frustration.

Now there's only one answer: We advertise our amazing lives on social media so everyone knows we're happy. How's life, you ask? I'm fucking crushing it. You say you're good? I'm *great*. Living the dream, baby.

The phrase "living the dream" has not been uttered in the past few years without an unhealthy dose of irony. These emerging patterns—fulfillment via materialism, filtered-to-perfection lives on social media, and advertising the accomplishments of our children as our own—drill even deeper into our friends' lives where the media can't touch, exacerbating the problem and feeding the parasite of externally derived goals, as we unintentionally do to our friends what they're unknowingly doing to us.

We're in this together, right? You believe it too, right?

We work near or beyond the limits of tolerance, expecting a prize at the end of a race, a reward that won't be there, that can't be there, because we're on the wrong road, taking the tollway but expecting the scenic route, mocking the idea of the "rat race" while our every step is dedicated to it. Still we wonder why we can't find fulfillment in the very things we've been promised *will* fulfill us, even though every one of us knows, going in, that we won't.

We wonder why we have nothing or, more accurately, why *everything* isn't enough, so let's ask the question.

Why not? Why isn't *everything* enough?

Everything isn't enough because we are taught to look outward, to drive for the trappings, the results, and the symptoms of happiness instead of drilling inward for the source, the wellspring, our individual fountainhead, which is where the kernels of fulfillment lie in wait, wondering if we'll ever stop watching television, turn off the radio, set down the phone, close the laptop, and look for them. *Everything*—in the material sense of it—is outside of you, and nothing external will bring you fulfillment.

Everything will never be enough if you define *everything* as what you have instead of *who you are*.

You don't need anything else to find fulfillment. Specifically, you can't buy anything else that will inch you closer to fulfillment. The meaning of life is not waiting for you in a pleasantly lit showroom, in your microbrew bubbles, or in your search-engine-optimized website. Marketing your personal brand will not unlock forgotten ancient secrets.

The crazy thing about our confusion between what we have and who we are is that we all know these things. If you take a second to consider the happiest times in your life, chances are they were with someone else, not something else. If you take an instant to whittle your life down to its most fulfilling moment so far, the odds are overwhelming it was in a moment of great challenge, and you succeeded in something you previously might have considered beyond your capabilities.

If we are most satisfied and most fulfilled when we're challenging ourselves, why do so many of us live our lives firmly ensconced within the limits of our abilities?

Why did I do it for so long?

Is it fear of failure? Is it that simple, or does the world around us—the world of undergraduate majors, career specificity, rigid resume formats, cubicles, and working lunches—discourage challenge and daring, politely yet firmly showing us which cubby is ours from elementary school through retirement? If you are not satisfied with the way the world works, what can you do? Bartend with your aeronautical design degree in your back pocket? Find an artist commune in Arizona? Bounce around through life, never fitting in? Revel in your quiet, public failure? Banish yourself to the land of misfit toys? What is there for you if you're not willing to pretend you're completely satisfied with the avenues to fulfillment our money-driven, accumulation-based society offers? Do you just play along and turn in your TPS reports?

Why do we expect more *stuff* to fill us to the brim with well-being? Do we really expect a new backpack to make it all okay? I don't think so. We know we don't need *more*. If anything, we need *less*. You're reading this because you know there's more to life. We mock our own consumption culture while it consumes us. We've even managed to make acting upon the feeling a cliché, calling it downsizing, living off the grid, or minimalism.

What does it get us? Nothing. All these bromides and clichés about what life is about are worthless if we don't act on them, and even then, sometimes taking action isn't enough. If you're slowly drowning in a sea of dissatisfaction, how long do you think a weekend "off the grid" will hold back the waves? Tuesday?

The issue is, even when we think about changing our lives, it's still in relation to what is outside: material possessions, time management, and email/cell phone habits.

This is a misunderstanding of what's important. A lot of us say we "hate" the news, "I don't do social media," or "I don't watch television." You don't have to give up TV to find fulfillment. You don't have to take a scythe to your social media pages to be happy. You don't have to give up your smartphone or stop perfecting your homemade root beer.

But you need to be aware that every time you click on a link or visit your social media page, you are likely moving further away from what will fulfill you, and you are wasting time you'll never get back.

Time passed is one thing you can never regain. If you're like most people, if you're like me, you've wasted the majority of your adult minutes allotted thus far and are further away from fulfillment than you were when you were a child. You can't recapture it, but beginning now, you can spend the time you have on what moves you rather than on what moves the economy.

You do not have to enslave yourself to meet quarterly expectations. It is not your obligation to sacrifice yourself to push the annual GDP over four percent.

To open yourself to finding the meaning of *your* life, translating that to purpose, and taking action on it so you experience daily fulfillment, you must shed yourself of external influences and standards, let go of the fear the media propagates, and ignore the constant, insidious pressure to buy more stuff. Stop trying to achieve someone else's ideal life.

But I gotta pay the bills.

Yes, you do. We're not shooting for a pauper's existence—our aim is a meaningful, fulfilling life—which may include oodles of coin. But your meaning and purpose must be determined in a vacuum of non-materialism. *After* you've done the hard work of discovering what moves you—without financial consideration—we'll turn your dusted-off and sharpened self-analysis skills to the question of how the hell you're going to make any money and succeed on *your* terms.

So first things first. We're off to a good start.

Now it's time to talk about religion.

GODS AND RELIGIONS

So Man Created God(s) In His Own Image

As WE SEARCH for life's meaning and purpose, it doesn't matter if God exists or not, but I think it's important to understand the purpose of gods and the nature of religion—the self-appointed earthly representatives of gods.

Throughout history, gods have represented what we didn't understand. As humanity gained control over the harvest, a god died. When people determined the sun was a star like all the other stars in the sky, a god died. During this long period of human history in which so many religions (now relegated to mythologies) featured pantheons of gods, there was a god to pray to or sacrifice to or fear for every natural occurrence and human trait.

Eventually we answered the basic questions of our lives. We developed the best methods of planting, nurturing, and harvesting crops. We (mostly/often/occasionally) took responsibility for our emotions and character flaws.

The day-to-day aspects of human existence and the natural world were, for the most part, explained. At the very least, we no longer ascribed our every victory or misfortune to the arbitrary whims of childish, angry gods who demanded bloody toys for favors.

But science still hadn't answered one crucial question, which people ask in different ways:

Why are we here?

What is the meaning of life?

What's the point of it all?

But why hasn't science answered these questions? We're all looking for our origin and what it means to exist. Shouldn't the answers be a scientific priority? Science can—or will someday—reveal the origin of life, as it has detailed the physics of moving bodies and the chemistry of explosives, but it won't reveal life's meaning or purpose. Science attempts to describe what exists and theorizes what might exist, not the internal, philosophical questions of existence.

That's up to us.

Meaning and purpose are unique to us all. These are deep, internal questions unanswerable without a systematic analysis of morals, values, experiences, and ideals. The basis for the meaning of your life lies in whatever is innate to you as an individual, combined with the sum of your experiences and directed by a handful of specific benchmark experiences. There is no all-encompassing, masses-inspiring meaning of life beyond the unsatisfactory answer of surviving long enough to procreate. Instead, there is the meaning of *your* life, and there is the meaning of *my* life, and rarely the twain shall meet.

As a consequence, the search for meaning is, by necessity, a solitary search. When the goal is personal fulfillment, it is *you* who must be fulfilled, not someone else, so all the answers must come from you. It requires more honesty with ourselves than most of us have experienced. You won't find enlightenment between the lines of ancient delusions. You won't find illumination within the whims of a jealous god.

You *will* find people taking it upon themselves to interpret the wants and requirements of an unknowable entity. But when you're looking to find meaning in life, something deeply resonant within you, the arbitrary interpretations of others can be crippling.

Consider the possibility you are failing or feel unfulfilled because your goals are in line with what you're told is expected of you, but not in line with who you are. Therefore, there is nothing behind your actions, nothing deep within you compelling you forward.

More and more each day, our society moves away from taking responsibility for oneself, and toward attaching blame to bad circumstances and others' actions or inactions. It's not far removed from blaming a drought on an angry rain god waiting for the dancing to begin. Accepting responsibility for yourself, your actions, your failures, and your future is a crucial step toward realizing fulfillment.

I don't know whether there is a God or if there have ever been gods. Our knowledge of our universe is partial at best. We can offer plausible explanations for a lot of the big things, but common sense tells us there's a lot more out there. Our technology will never be advanced enough to see it all, know it all, or overpower the impressive natural forces at work on earth or beyond.

That said, there are specific aspects of religion that make finding real meaning and purpose difficult, and genuine fulfillment impossible, if you're unwilling to suspend your belief and think for yourself:

- Religion's position that people are incapable of moralizing for themselves, and without the threat of eternal fiery punishment the world would descend into chaos, mass slaughters, and war
- Religion's foundation that people are evil by nature and are born that way

Do we need religion to convey to us the Golden Rule, which can be found in almost everyone's everyday behavior? Do the Ten Commandments represent the height of our ethical philosophy? I don't think so. Yet too many base their morality on the worldviews of people who lived thousands of years ago, people whose knowledge of the world did not rival a modern first grader.

Most people are, by nature, good. Well-known research by Karen Wynn and Paul Bloom at Yale University's "Baby Lab" indicates babies are born with a sense of right and wrong. A baby is not a blank slate or "a perfect idiot," as Jean-Jacques Rousseau called them in 1762. Evidently, we are born with a sense of morality, which indicates any thinking person can self-moralize and does not need religion to dictate the simple wisdom and behavioral tenets that form the basis of civilization.

The Golden Rule and other basic moral standards of human interaction might be ingrained within us.

As you search for your life's meaning and purpose, the question becomes this: Do ancient codes encouraging you to surrender responsibility and control of your life to a supernatural entity help or hinder you?

The Disconnect

The disconnect between your purpose in life and religion's purpose for you exists because religion and other afterlife-believing faiths/cults/systems position death as the threshold between what we know to be real and what we want to be real, though thinking individuals understand life after death is a distraction from the greater challenge of creating and contributing while alive.

What began with the first origin stories—based on what our ancestors *didn't* know about the physical world—has slow-dissolved to our current origin stories, which someday will join their forerunners in the category of mythology. Yet we cling to them, struggling onward with intentional ignorance of what we *do* know about our past, our biology, our world, and the universe at large.

Religion's domination of "meaning" hamstrings humanity by framing our existence in ancient, archaic superstition and creation myths, which we have failed to dismiss as such. This has resulted in legions searching for something outside themselves and beyond reality yet finding only promises of something after death that manifests itself—in life—as a hole that must be filled.

That *hole* is the real meaning in your life and day-to-day purpose. Like drugs, alcohol, and other addictions, religion fills the hole in many people. Is it any wonder religion often replaces alcohol and drugs for people with so-called addictive personalities?

People have always created the gods in their image to explain the mysteries of existence, fusing the passions of people and the chaos of nature to create personalities and answer the question *Why am I here?* externally, eliminating the need to consider the nature, possibilities, or meaning of life so long as you have faith.

But life's true reality is life itself, as opposed to faith in something after death, something uncertain and unknowable—a phantom goal.

Is this a goal upon which we should base our lives? Should we trust our fulfillment to others' delusions?

To experience fulfillment, you must let go of fear and embrace the idea that this life is what you get. *This* life. Life here and now *is* the experience, and fulfillment is possible through the discovery of the meaning of your life and the subsequent pursuit of purpose, not through religious delusion and irrational promises. Once you've abandoned religion as a structure by which to frame your life, there is nothing to cloud or diminish the reality, preciousness, and awe of your existence.

Suppression versus Expression

I propose that you and I are perfectly capable of creating our own moral code. Given the opportunity, which we are every day, we would almost certainly agree upon basic standards of existence and interpretations of right and wrong. Freed from the grip of religion and its governmental minions, our morals and ethics would be more in line with our nature.

The structure of religion and other external sources is the

suppression neatly contained in the word *don't*. In most interpretations of the Ten Commandments, all ten are "thou shalt not" in nature. Yet when people consider what they want to do with their lives, the conflict is packed like the singularity before the Big Bang in the tiny word *do*. *Do* is a verb, an expression, an action.

It is unworkable to allow religion to interpret life's meaning for you. Via the nature of its stated objective, religion marginalizes life by working for and glorifying an afterlife, which makes life on earth something to be maneuvered and endured, not defined and lived.

The alternative to religion, the alternative that enables you to find real meaning and purpose in life, is to hold *yourself* as the highest authority of your own morality, behavior, and endeavors. By examining your life, your sense of right and wrong, and your unique passions and experiences, you can develop a far more effective framework within which to live meaningfully.

FRIENDS AND FAMILY

They Love You and Want the Best for You, But…

WHEN I DETERMINED what the meaning of my life was, the reactions of my friends and family surprised me. In the past, I'd skirted around the idea, as well as its solution, arguing with friends, soapboxing, and grandstanding. I hadn't recognized how much it meant to me or that I was willing to not only dedicate my life to fighting *against* something but to also, perhaps more crucially, find a way to solve the problem. Because of the nature of people striving to be *more* (essentially, the sort of person who would read this book), fighting for or against something by discovering or inventing a problem's solution is a common—and excellent—strategy. If you're looking for meaning and purpose in your life, chances are you won't be satisfied with just complaining. You'll want to solve the problem.

Once I was certain of the problem, its meaning, and my proposed solution, I started talking about it to the people most important to me.

I expected significant resistance or blasé nods.

That wasn't what happened. Granted, it wasn't overwhelming, enthusiastic support either, but reading between the lines of the questions I was asked, I could tell what I was saying made sense to my family. Questions from my friends told me I'd stumbled onto something many of them struggled with themselves. Some thought they might give it a go, while a few admitted they were too lazy to go through the process I proposed during the early stages of writing this book.

Through their reactions, I developed some ideas on the motivations, reservations, and enthusiasm of friends and family.

Your friends and family, no matter how much they love you, won't be as fired up about the "new you" as you wish they would be. Sure, your parents want you to succeed, but it's more accurate to say they want you to succeed within a definition of success they and others will recognize (attributable to good parenting). This enables your parents to feel they've raised you right. If your fulfillment doesn't result in the usual socially acceptable and—maybe more importantly—*visible* trappings of success (power, prestige, money, minions), don't expect much more than the forbearing nods you received as a child.

Outstanding success and happiness often meets with resistance from family and friends. Family members, particularly siblings, can be resentful of astounding success and new paths.

Why? Great question. Maybe it puts a bright light on what they are (or aren't) doing with their lives, highlights any self-perceived failings, or brings into focus the unhappiness so many people experience every day. Maybe it's easier for people to relate to others with the same frustrations, failings, and small successes.

With friends, it's much the same. Your friends love you for who you are, not who you want to be or who you become. That's comforting in many ways, but not so much when you're trying to do more with your life. Many celebrities have commented on the difficulty of maintaining longtime friendships after fame strikes. Jealousy and insecurity put in long hours trying to dismantle even the closest friendship.

Does this apply with inner success and the resulting visible fulfillment you'll experience? It might.

When you succeed in finding your purpose in life and pursue it, it demonstrates such a life is possible and such fulfillment is attainable, and it poses unspoken questions to all who know you.

"What am I doing with my life?"

"What is the thing I'm working so hard for?"

"Does what I'm doing mean anything or matter to anyone?"

Unfortunately, unless they're looking for something themselves, these are questions most people don't want to face. But wouldn't the world be a better place if everyone faced them and then acted?

On a personal level, I found my dislike for the taste of alcohol—and consequent nondrinker status—made some people uncomfortable, resulting in countless conversations about why I don't drink, accompanied by disbelief, skeptical looks, and suspicions of an alcoholic past.

If something as trivial as drinking habits can drive people apart, how can someone living a life of deliberate purpose, fueled by knowledge of the meaning of their own life, expect to be embraced by anyone who, to that point, has been working for the weekend?

Be An Example

Given so many people go through life without examining their meaning and determining their purpose, instead living through the haze of routine, performing jobs below their abilities, and using happy hours to brighten unhappy days, discovering someone close to them has worked to determine what life means—and is now pursuing it—can be unsettling and unwelcome.

"Good for you," comes the tidy reply.

By being an example of what is possible, you spotlight others' shortcomings or lack of motivation, and some might resent you for your success, causing your friendships and family relationships to evolve.

That's one way it could go.

Another possibility is your search for meaning will motivate your family and friends, and friends of friends, to look inside themselves and be more than they are now, on *their* terms.

Is there a solution? You likely want to keep your friends. It's better to have good relationships with your family. You want your parents to be proud of you, feel good about their parenting, and so on. How can you stack the odds in your favor? How do you affect those closest to you positively instead of incurring resentment?

Although the reactions of others are out of your control—as are their internal dialogues, visceral reactions, insecurities, victories, disappointments, and motivations—there are a few things you can do to influence others positively:

- As you're transforming from an externally influenced person to someone with self-derived meaning, accept the idea you *could* serve as a role model for someone in your inner circle if the person perceives you in that way. The first step is *always* you.
- Remember that by encouraging others to find their meaning and purpose in life and to follow through on it, you are improving the world as a whole, helping those closest to you to live fulfilling lives, and enriching your friendships. But all you can do is encourage. Your friends and family will have to do their own heavy lifting, just as you will.
- Resist the evangelizing so common when we discover something new we believe in. Instead, provide clear answers when asked what's making such a difference in your life. Lead by example. Suggest others consider what is meaningful to them. Their path to fulfillment won't be the same as yours, because their experiences, beliefs, values, and ideals are different than yours, even if you

grew up in the same house. All you can do is tell them what you've experienced and point the way.

To Sum It Up

We are overwhelmingly influenced and shaped by the messages we hear and see every day, the people closest to us, and the cultural stories and expectations we learned while growing up. Most of us are dependent upon our parents well past the point our worldview is formed. To compound the indoctrination, we're steered toward the values and beliefs of whatever religion we are born into. Concurrently, we're immersed in pop culture via television, cinema, advertising, and the internet. It's easy to see why the standards of our environment preempt most of us from considering the possibility other measures of "success" may exist.

Even now, with the benefits of an adult mind and easy access to differing perspectives, the questions persist:

- Who am I to wonder if following in my father's footsteps is the right path for me?
- Who am I to question religion's right to define meaning?
- Who am I to ask if money is an accurate measure of happiness and if more money will fulfill me?
- Who am I to suggest there is a better way?

Acknowledging that your friends and family, religion, gurus of all stripes, and the world's media, marketing, and retail machines exert tremendous influence upon how we see value and fulfillment is the first step toward answering these questions with empowering, productive, rhetorical questions:

- Why am I allowing my life to be plotted for me?
- Why am I allowing someone else to dictate my values and morals?

- Why am I agreeing that the sole standard of success and fulfillment is money?
- Why am I not forging my own path?

Once you shed external influences, you may be surprised by what you determine means the most to you in life and what you're willing to fight for or against. The answers to the important questions—*What is the meaning of life?* and *Why am I here?*—have always been inside you, waiting for you to find them.

Soon you'll begin a step-by-step process during which you'll ask yourself the right questions to evolve from who you are now to who you want to be:

- Meaning: You'll determine what means the most to you, the thing toward which your life (to this point) has led.
- Purpose: You'll choose to "fight" (my term, maybe not yours) for or against (sometimes both) the unique meaning of your life.
- Living the life: You'll begin pursuing your purpose.
- Fulfillment: You'll learn to understand how fulfillment feels and how to maintain it throughout life.

Each step builds upon the last. The first—discovering and defining the meaning of your life—provides the foundation for a fulfilling life. Meaning will inform everything you do, provide context for your most important decisions, and fuel your purpose. Without meaning, life can seem pointless and unfulfilling. If you want to lead a fulfilling life, first determine its meaning.

So let's get to it.

PART
TWO

PART TWO
THE MEANING OF LIFE

Meaning is not a rudder, a map, or a route. It's not a result or an end. It's a beginning. Determining the meaning of your life builds the foundation for your life. Your actions flow from it. Your decisions are based upon it. Meaning is your singularity.

WHAT IS THE MEANING OF LIFE?

What Isn't the Meaning of Life?

WHAT IS the meaning of life? There are a few stock answers:

- Live a life based on religious tenets so you can go to heaven, be reincarnated, etc.
- Procreate.
- Be good to others.

More recently, other ideas have entered the fray:

- Follow your bliss/passion/whims.
- Just love.

Which one is right? It's important to procreate, at least for our species (maybe not so much for you and me—we're already here). Being good to others is better than the alternative. "Follow your bliss" and "just love" are wonderful on bumper stickers. Adhering to religious tenets so you can go to heaven could be interpreted as part delusion and part procrastination.

None of the current attempts at defining the meaning of life are good enough. None of the ideas go deep enough.

The Achilles' heel of most pronouncements of life's meaning is that they are efforts at universal application, and they fail to account for time's passage, cultural progression, and individual interpretations of life. There are thousands of cheeses. There are thousands of wines. There are millions of songs. If we can't settle on which *water* tastes best, doesn't that indicate there are massive differences in how each of us sees the world? Isn't there *anything* we can agree upon?

Laws, regulations, and commandments work (some better than others) to establish and maintain an ordered, civil society. They reflect the values of an entire society or at least the leaders' interpretation of their society's values.

But laws can't confer meaning to an individual.

The purpose of law is a peaceful, orderly society. Law doesn't—and can't—define you, what you value, or how you see the world. Are you going to find the meaning of life within tort law? Are there secrets to existence written between the lines of swimming pool regulations?

How about the big three monotheistic holy books? At best, the world's religions are the creation stories of ancient peoples struggling to make sense of their world. At worst, the major monotheisms intentionally devalue the life experience. Blindly following the direction of ancient mystics, books, and charlatans pushes you no closer to a fulfilling life. Basing your life on the superstitions and ravings of people ignorant of the most basic natural laws demonstrates a considerable reluctance to think for yourself.

What Is the Meaning of Life?

The meaning of life is a difficult question with as many answers and subtleties as there are people in the world. Fortunately, there is likely only one answer for you, and for our purposes, it is the only answer that matters. Still, determining the meaning of your life requires deep, considered, ordered thought.

For meaning to *drive* anything, it must be unique to you. There is no single answer to the question that's satisfying for all, but there is one sure way to get there. Unlike in ancient times, all roads do not lead to Rome. Rather, one road leads to many destinations.

This is one of the most important realizations to embrace. The meaning of life is different for everyone, even close friends or family members. Once you determine the meaning of your life, you shouldn't expect your best friend to exclaim, "Eureka! That *is* the meaning of life." You're not looking for confirmation from others. You're driving for internal certainty. Defining the meaning of your life is the only way to live a fulfilling life based in reality.

That's not what you usually hear.

Generally, it's assumed the meaning of life is "one size fits all" by design, as if there should be one meaning for everyone. But if we all possess individual consciousness, can the most elemental philosophical aspect of existence be uniform?

It is not *the* meaning of life. It is not *a* meaning of life. It is the meaning of *your* life.

A meaningful life is grounded in reality and the world we see and must live in, not blind hope for something beyond life, something unknown, metaphysical, or spiritual, something for which you have to subsume your goals and desires for empty promises that are nothing more than fragile fortifications against the fear of nonexistence.

To have a direct relationship with a creative force would be comforting, but one of the most important steps you can take is to accept that this life is the beginning and the end and will be your sole experience of reality. This is the only time you get.

It falls to each of us to recognize that self-determined meaning is life's only valid meaning.

To determine the meaning of your life and develop what flows from that determination, stop *believing* and start *thinking*.

Unfortunately, our culture's priorities don't include individual philosophical examination—at least beyond those put forth by Madison Avenue's best minds, who daily present compelling cases that my choice of car brand defines me as a human being.

Knowing the meaning of your life simplifies, clarifies, and crystallizes. It makes the right choices obvious and the others superfluous. Understanding your life's meaning and purpose stills the noise and chatter, leaving internal quiet and certainty.

By first determining meaning and defining purpose, using your inner perspective (self) as opposed to an outer perspective (gods, gurus, friend or family expectations, cultural standards of success), you can unify yourself with a common purpose and live a meaningful life.

That said, the determination of meaning can be difficult and emotional if you're honest with yourself. At times, it can seem as if there is no end to the "yes, but why?" aspect of the process, much like letting your inner five-year-old run roughshod through your mind. But if you agree that a few days of self-analysis are better than a lifetime of guesswork and frustration, it's easy to see how delving deep to find the meaning of your life, based on your experiences and impressions, is the best and most direct way to achieve fulfillment.

FINDING THE MEANING IN YOUR LIFE

Put the Y to You

GURUS TALK about the necessity of asking "positive" questions, with the idea that phrasing something positively will stop you from beating up on yourself.

I've put in a lot of time with gurus over the years via their books, tapes, and seminars. Some were more effective than others, but I didn't move forward until I stopped blindly accepting myself as okay, stopped blaming everyone else for my lack of fulfillment, and asked far-reaching negative questions:

What's wrong with me?

What am I doing wrong?

Why can't I find something I'm happy doing?

Once I began asking negative questions and tore myself down (ironically, like a coach will do when working with a gifted athlete with poor mechanics), I was able to get to the attitudinal flaws, misperceptions, and vagueness about what I wanted from life—and what life offers—that had held me back. Once I asked what were considered the "wrong" questions, I was able to get to the right answers.

One of these was my belief I had been screwed out of a professional baseball career, an apparent conspiracy among my college coaches. Coaches whose jobs depended upon winning had kept their best chance of winning (me) off the field in order to—what? Put that way, it sounds pretty stupid. It is, but these are the things we tell ourselves to rationalize our lack of success when, for what we perceive as self-preservation purposes, we must find something, *anything*, at fault for our failures.

"You're uncoachable."

It took years of maturation, and my brother's thunderclap pronouncement, for me to see it, but eventually I had to accept that, in my life, and in baseball, I was the problem. As I'm writing this, I'm realizing my coaches did everything they could to find a place for me in the lineup, but even if you can hit the hell out of the ball, if you're an uncoachable know-it-all with an average arm who transforms every pop fly into a circus, you're not going to play at the highest levels. I guaran-goddamn-tee it.

In the love arena, if you have a continuing string of failed relationships, and you are the only common factor, guess who the problem is?

Who sees this at any moment other than in retrospect?

It took a few days for "you're uncoachable" and other choice, charged, unedited sibling evaluations to sink in. In those admittedly dark, thrilling days, I burnt the bridges to my excuses for failure and arrived at the liberating conclusion I've mentioned: If I am the problem, I'm also the solution. Though you can't control how others react or how external forces respond to your actions, you *are* in total control of what you think and do.

Though there are situations in which randomness and tragedy conspire against some people, it is far more likely *you* are your problem, just as I was my problem. Via laziness, lack of vision, or what-should-I-do-itis, you have managed to do less with your life than you could have—so far.

A Few Questions

Let's begin with questions of the negative sort. Though later in this book you'll write down your answers to questions of morality, values, and ideals, my intent for these first questions is to warm you to the honest self-analysis you'll need to determine your life's meaning and purpose. At this stage, there's no need to write down your answers if you don't want to.

Honest answers—*real* answers—to these questions can be difficult, so spend some time on each question before moving to the next:

Is an element of my personality or character preventing me from succeeding?

Is a set of beliefs preventing me from living meaningfully?

WHAT HAVE I done with my life so far? Describe your personal and professional choices.

WHY HAVEN'T I found something I'm happy doing? What's the disconnect between what you've done and what's meaningful to you?

HAVE my choices aligned with who I am? If not, why not?

Now you have a few attitudinal and character insights, but what can you do with them? It's nigh on impossible to change your character. In practice, I think it would play out as living a false life. I would be getting along, playing at being "coachable," but it wouldn't be me. Is that all we want, to get along? No. We want more. We want to *be* more, but how can we accomplish the vague idea of being more within reality's boundaries? For example, I can't go on some self-discovery walkabout. I have children. Money is necessary for purchasing goods and services, and therefore necessary to support my family.

For years I'd failed to see something important in that last sentence about money. But enough had changed inside me that I understood there was a problem with how I looked at money. I'd spent a lot of time changing jobs, working on side businesses, always trying to hit it big and make a lot of money so I could... so I could... what?

So I wouldn't have to do anything anymore.

Even now I wonder what that would have looked like. I'd work as little as possible so I could lounge about the rest of the time, I suppose. I would manifest "automated internet income" so I could live life as a perpetual vacation. Was I imagining a beach? I lived in Southern California for over twenty years, but I rarely went to the beach. Was I so brainwashed as to what a "dream life" was that I couldn't recognize how little of it corresponded with who *I* was?

That wasn't being more. That wasn't living with meaning and purpose. If anything, that was being less and living less. I was doing things in which I had no interest to make so much money I wouldn't have to do anything ever again.

I guess it sounded like a good idea at the time.

How do you view money? Do you look forward to no longer

having to work? Do you yearn to invent something that will set you up for a lifetime of leisure?

If so, I urge you to reconsider.

A life of leisure is not a worthy goal if you have anything worthwhile to contribute. But what is worthwhile? That is one of the questions that led to this book.

What is worthwhile?

Again, a deeply personal question only you can answer. Value is unique to each of us. When you do something that *means something to you*, it becomes more than a job or a business card or a promotion. *You* become more than a father or mother or employee or friend. Consider becoming a symbol, an inspiration to others. You could be what's *right* with the world.

Once you decide what is worthwhile and understand what you can contribute, you will see the dehumanizing flaws in our culture's foundation. We know society is not set up for billions of purposeful individuals on unique paths, living fulfilling lives. Civilization is an engine of sorts, with each of us filling roles that contribute to an ever-expanding economy with the promise of eternal life after death in a heaven free from money, hard labor, busy work, stress, bills, and advertising—an everlasting White Ball in which we dance and fornicate to a trance music-infused angelic chorus. If you use the interpretations of television and film as your guide, heaven is like earth but without the elements we *know* diminish the human experience.

Those diminishing elements exist because working for material wealth, marrying and having children, and ascending to heaven are the tent poles of our cultural story. Together, they reduce us to meek little cogs of commerce, living now for things we know don't matter and later for something we know doesn't exist.

Is it any wonder we eat everything in sight and buy whatever's being sold?

The cultural story discussed in earlier chapters does not die easily, nor do the stories we tell ourselves about ourselves. Our personal stories are revisionist history, bent on keeping us firmly—and necessarily—in the protagonist's role, populating the world's stage with random antagonists and foils. To succeed, to live a fulfilling life, disregard the cultural story and rewrite *your* story. Ask yourself about the real value of accumulating things, question the idea of living to achieve a *life of abundance*, of the necessity of earning more money, of working within an externally influenced profession.

These questions are important because if you're unfulfilled, it's unlikely the problem is that you don't have enough stuff or that you're $25,000 short on salary. It's that you've probably taken the path of least resistance, doing what you're expected to do or can easily do, and have lived a life unexamined. You're working hard for stuff that won't make you any happier and goals that won't fulfill you or make anyone respect or love you more. The objectives set for you by your culture satisfy cultural needs, not yours.

We spend our lives—an all-too-quick succession of high school counselor meetings, college majors, "productive" years, retirement, and twilight—wondering what we should do with our lives.

Instead of asking yourself *what you should do*, ask yourself *who you should be*.

The Search for Meaning Is an Inner Search

Meaning must be discovered and defined (mined, if you will) within before it can be manifested in an outward way.

By maintaining the search for meaning as an "inner" search, the objective of life becomes self-defined, limitless in possibility, and unique to you. There is nothing you must believe or buy to grasp the meaning of your life. There is no place for fear. The meaning of your life is yours from the start. There is nothing to save you from, no hole that must be filled, no faith to be misplaced. You are your own self-contained entity.

An external search for meaning, such as salvation, a newer car, better kitchen furniture, or a bigger house creates a disconnect with reality. None of these will fulfill you in a permanent way. None of these will make you happier than any other object or faith-based destination. None will fill you with purposeful action fueled by clear knowledge of the meaning of your life.

With an inner search for meaning, there is no disconnect with reality. The search for meaning and purpose is self-contained, of a piece, guidable by you, and available to you if you're willing to think for yourself. Fulfillment is attainable in the real world during your lifetime, springing from your thoughts and through your purposeful actions.

In that way, the inner search for meaning is something you must earn. You can't shout, "I believe!" each Sunday and be done with it. There's no deathbed Hail Mary. Once the inner search is complete and you've determined the meaning of your life, it's up to you to take action on it. It's up to you to do what's necessary for your fulfillment.

Real-world meaning is discovered and developed, revised and refined, over the course of a lifetime. It is unique to you, and only you can determine what thing, issue, need, or action moves you intellectually and emotionally. Only you have experienced your life. Only *you* have seen all you have seen. We are each our own sun around which all others orbit. This is a result of individual consciousness. To deny this is folly and an avoidance.

To use it is a different proposition altogether. Using your individual consciousness, your unique worldview, as the basis for your actions lifts the shroud and casts a clarifying light on everything around you.

Perform a slash-and-burn on your illusions, delusions, excuses, negativity, and false positivity. Simultaneously, tune out external influences and dismiss cultural expectations. Ask yourself what you value, what you will fight for, and what you can surrender, all while understanding that, with few exceptions, you must still live in your culture and there are only a few quick, unfortunate steps between idealistic and homeless.

Why Am I? is *not* about giving up your earthly possessions. It's about deciding which earthly possessions you need and which ones you don't. It's *not* about getting in touch with the universe and encountering your spirit animal. It's about determining who you are, who you want to be, and how to get there. It's *not* about removing yourself from society and finding an abandoned cabin in which to write your manifesto. It's about removing yourself from the cultural engine so you can recognize it for what it is and how it has influenced your entire life.

To remove yourself from the cultural engine, you must free yourself from the cultural story. In the next few chapters, you'll develop your Moral Code. A self-derived, written Moral Code, even if identical to your culture's accepted morals, is a crucial step in determining the meaning of your life.

SELF-MORALIZATION

What Is Morality?

MORALITY IS DEFINED as the principles concerning the distinction between right and wrong. Therefore, whether you are a moral person in others' eyes is based on your behavior (and how you say something, if we consider political correctness) compared to your culture's accepted moral code.

The problem with the accepted moral codes of most cultures is they are usually based upon religious principles that begin with the supposition people are inherently evil.

Are we? I've met few people I'd categorize as "evil," and often their "evilness" stemmed from their opposition to my actions and my inability to see beyond what I wanted. Good, kind people have populated the vast majority of my life.

But religion propagandizes the evil of humanity, particularly the evil of those who do not believe exactly what *we* believe.

The moral codes of religion and superstition have managed to deliver to the world the Inquisition and countless "witch trials," yet we still cling to the ideas upon which these atrocities were based. Our religion-based moral codes assume people are fundamentally guilty, yet our laws begin with people being presumed innocent.

Why the 180-degree contradiction between the assumptions of religion and law? Because religions are structured superstition, while a legal system—regardless of whether we agree with a particular law—is systematized reason.

Why do we persist in accepting religious moral systems that fail to meet the standards of our most basic legal philosophy? Why do we embrace our collective demons yet resist our individual minds?

Why are parents more likely to stop their children from watching simulated sex in a movie but not simulated murder, particularly when sex is necessary for the continuance of the species as the first act for creating life, and violence (as presented on TV and in movies) is usually the end of a life and tends to show the worst of human behavior?

The sex and violence reversal is particularly interesting because it infers our most natural act as humans (creating life, the thing we need to survive as a species) is something to be ashamed of and that the most unnatural, abhorrent act (violently ending another's life) is to be glamorized and promoted. Is it self-hate? Are we ashamed of ourselves, or is it something deeper?

These are puzzling questions when considering that people are, from the beginning and for the most part, good. As mentioned previously, Yale University's "Baby Lab" has determined we are born with an innate morality, that babies overwhelmingly prefer the good guy over the bad guy, and an immoral baby (if you can make the leap to calling a baby "immoral" when he or she prefers a "mean" puppet to a "nice" puppet) is the rare exception. From birth, we are able to self-moralize and self-ethicize despite our ignorance of supernatural wrath's looming threat.

Why do we accept these contradictions to our very nature?

We've accepted them because we've accepted religion's assertion that we are bad from birth. Despite university-level, clinical, double-blind evidence to the contrary, we *believe* we are flawed and in need of guidance beyond ourselves.

We have—to this point—quietly adopted common morality as our own morality. Blindly accepting (and crediting) a moral code—based on superstition forged in an ignorant, barbaric, ancient world—as the foundation on which to build your life is no way to find real meaning in your life.

Moral Compass?

One of the first steps to determining the meaning of your life is separating yourself from external influence and developing your own Moral Code. Once developed, how you live your life follows from your Moral Code. It will serve as both guide and boundaries while determining the meaning of your life.

Often you will find the meaning of your life within your self-determined morality, because morality is derived from innate knowledge and learned principles (such as the natural wrongness of murder), and we tend to passionately hold to these greater truths and guidelines about existence.

We're often presented with the phrase "moral compass." Because the meaning of life is so intertwined with what you see as right and wrong, and because universally accepted morality is based upon someone else's values and perspective, without your own moral code you will default to an externally based perspective. This is why so many of us go through life feeling as if something is missing and life should be *more*. We're basing our lives on what's most important to everyone else. There's no basis to our actions and nothing to refer to that is undeniably ours.

Your Moral Code informs the meaning of your life, which provides the foundation of your purpose. Your actions are a reflection, or confirmation, of your Moral Code. Thinking and acting in alignment with a self-developed Moral Code is effortless. If you are honest with yourself when determining your values and developing your unique Moral Code, there will be no struggle to live "morally." You will embody your Moral Code. Living otherwise would be unnatural.

I recommend developing a Moral Code with positive statements (*I will*) in addition to the inevitable negative statements (*I won't*, unless you want to go archaic and use *thou shalt* and *thou shalt not*). By beginning with the premise that you are born good, in direct opposition to the idea of humanity's inherent evilness, you'll quietly strike a blow for sanity and reason.

It's tempting to offer my own Moral Code as an example. However, displaying my Moral Code would be yet one more external influence you would have to discard. Instead, I have provided guidelines and questions to help you develop your own.

Since you were born, you've been able to distinguish right from wrong. While developing your Moral Code, remember to include the "right" with the "wrong." Knowing what to do is as important as knowing what not to do.

YOUR MORAL CODE

Question Everything

Your Moral Code is the first of three codes you'll develop as you determine the meaning of your life. Your Values Code and your Ideals Code will follow logically and naturally from your Moral Code. After each question that follows, I've left space for you to write your answers. If you would prefer not to write in this book or if you have the e-book or audiobook, you can download the PDF of the questions at tewhitaker.com.

The questions encourage you to examine your thoughts, experiences, beliefs, attitudes, and behaviors. There are both positive questions and negative questions. Once you've completed the questions, you will build your "formal" Moral Code by keeping what is important and discarding what is not.

In developing your Moral Code, ask yourself if your answers reflect what you *really* think or what you are *supposed* to think. Choose the former, and guard against the latter. Often, your ideas of right and wrong will be, justifiably, in lockstep with what we all think. Other times, not so much. To determine the true meaning of your life, it's crucial that your Moral Code is *yours*.

Moral Code Questions

For each question, there is space for eight answers. I chose eight for several reasons, and because eight is not ten.

WHAT ARE the core behaviors everyone must follow for individuals to interact peacefully?
 1.
 2.
 3.
 4.
 5.
 6.
 7.
 8.

TURN these core behaviors into positive statements (I will).
 1.
 2.
 3.
 4.
 5.
 6.
 7.
 8.

WHAT BEHAVIORS must everyone avoid for individuals to interact peacefully?

1.
2.
3.
4.
5.
6.
7.
8.

TURN these behaviors into negative statements (I will not).

1.
2.
3.
4.
5.
6.
7.
8.

WHAT BEHAVIORS ARE necessary for humanity to adopt to continue forward (biologically, technologically, environmentally, etc.) not only for survival but for the advancement of our species and/or world?

1.
2.
3.
4.
5.

6.

7.

8.

TURN THESE INTO POSITIVE STATEMENTS.

1.

2.

3.

4.

5.

6.

7.

8.

WHAT BEHAVIORS MUST **humanity avoid so that we can continue forward (biologically, technologically, environmentally, etc.) without destroying our species and/or world?**

1.

2.

3.

4.

5.

6.

7.

8.

TURN THESE INTO NEGATIVE STATEMENTS.

1.

2.

3.
4.
5.
6.
7.
8.

ARE you passionate about any of the above behaviors—positive or negative? Which ones?

1.
2.
3.
4.
5.
6.
7.
8.

TURN these into positive or negative statements, based on their nature.

1.
2.
3.
4.
5.
6.
7.
8.

Build Your Moral Code

Review your positive or negative statements as well as the raw answers that helped you craft your positive and negative statements. Using these statements as principles, build your Moral Code with the principles you consider absolutes. There is no right or wrong number of principles. If you need more room, download the PDF at the web address previously provided.

1.

2.

3.

4.

5.

6.

7.

8.

9.

10.

11.

12.

13.

14.

15.

16.

17.

18.

19.

20.

21.

22.

23.

24.

CONGRATULATIONS. You have created your Moral Code.

YOUR VALUES CODE

What Is a Values Code?

For our purposes, values are the things in your world or the world at large that you deem crucial in either a positive or negative light. Therefore, your Values Code is a collection of your specific thoughts about what is right and wrong with the world.

Whereas your Moral Code is comprised of the core behaviors you deem necessary for life to flourish on both individual and societal levels, your Values Code is your evaluation of the world's current state, with your accompanying view on its rightness or wrongness.

Hijacking Your Mind

Though we're encouraged to suffer the world's paper cuts, you don't have to immerse yourself in things unlikely to touch your life. Unfortunately, cable networks and internet outlets—desperate to fill a vacuum threatening to collapse into a dense, dangerous mass of independent thought and considered opinion—pummel your brain with today's atrocities and outrages and tragedies, tomorrow's doomsday predictions and mega-sales, and an infinite string of heartwarming bubble gum fuzziness.

Breaking free from the drivel is a feat on the order of escaping the earth's orbit.

So how do you ignore what you're told to care about and determine what you do, in fact, actually, legitimately, care about? Where does passion live? What stays with you? How do you know if you really *do* care about the heroic struggles of Iowa soybean farmers, as opposed to being a victim of media inundation?

You question everything.

What are they trying to sell to me? What's the motivation behind this message? Are the Vegans defeating the Dairy Council's relentless public service announcements, or are eggs healthy this month?

You practice vigorous self-awareness.

Why am I doing this? Is what I'm doing contributing to my life, or wasting it? Do I mean what I'm saying right now? Am I wearing these clever, unexpected, colorful, graphic socks because they reveal the internal me, or because I'm a slave to whatever I'm told is hip?

You build your opinions from facts.

Do I think this because it's true, or because I'm told it's true? Who are the real experts on this topic? Where can I find an unbiased account? Do the liberals really want my guns, or are the NRA and the gun manufacturers banking on social entropy and anarchy as a business model?

You decide for *yourself*.

Values Code Questions

After each values question, I've left space for you to write your answers. If you prefer not to write in this book or you have the e-book or audiobook, you can download the PDF of the questions at tewhitaker.com.

The questions encourage you to examine your thoughts, experiences, beliefs, and attitudes in relation to the state of our world.

There are both positive questions and negative questions. Some of the questions and your answers will intersect. The idea is to more fully illuminate your thoughts on the state of the world and why you think and feel the way you do. Once you've completed the questions, you will build your "formal" Values Code by keeping what is important and discarding what's not.

In developing your Values Code, ask yourself if your answers reflect how you *really* see the world or if you are repeating what you've heard or read. Don't be lazy. It's important your answers reflect what you think, not what someone else believes.

WHAT IS RIGHT with the world/your country/life? Why?

WHAT IS wrong with the world/your country/life? Why?

WHAT ABOUT THE WORLD/YOUR country/life is unfair? Why? Is it hardwired into existence, or could it be changed?

WHAT EXCITES you about the world/your country/life? What can't you shut up about? Why?

DOES ANYTHING ABOUT THE WORLD/YOUR country/life make you angry or want to cry? Why?

WHAT IS MISSING in the world/your country/life that, if you willed it into existence with a snap of your fingers,

would make everything better for everybody? Why is it missing?

Build Your Values Code

Review your evaluations of the world's (and *your* world's) current state. Simplify your evaluations into sweeping statements of right and wrong such as *It's right that...* or *It's wrong that...* or something similar. Make your statements as emotionally or intellectually charged as you wish. Though much is right and wrong with the world, there is no right or wrong way to write your Values Code, and no required length so long as it's clear to you. If you need more room, download the PDF at the web address previously provided.

1.
2.
3.
4.
5.
6.
7.
8.
9.
10.
11.
12.
13.
14.
15.
16.

CONGRATULATIONS. You have built your Values Code.

YOUR IDEALS CODE

What Is an Ideals Code?

Your Ideals Code is how you think the world should be. It is developed in reference to your Moral Code and Values Code.

Examining your Codes brings into focus the compromises, conflicts, and consistencies you see in the world, both right and wrong (Values Code) and the behaviors of yourself and others on both personal and societal levels (Moral Code). In turn, this comparison enables you to build a picture of how the world is versus how the world *should be* (Ideals Code).

A good Ideals Code describes specific elements of a realistic utopia—the elements most important to you—in either their current utopian state or how they would be in a perfect world.

How many times have you thought or said something like "If I could snap my fingers" or "In a perfect world" or started a sentence with "Ideally"? Now's your chance to write it down and do something about it. Every invention to improve our lives, every good and right society, every push toward equality and fairness began with an idealistic thought, action, or demand. Idealism is not something we should praise or cynically smirk at or admire. It's something we should *act upon.*

Build Your Ideals Code

Take your Moral Code and compare it to your habits and behaviors, and the habits/behaviors of most people. Do the same with your Values Code and the state of the world.

What's right in the world? What's not?

If something doesn't correspond with your Moral Code, or you see a sweeping negative statement in your Values Code—these are possibilities for change. Use these inconsistencies between what *is* and what *should be* to inform your description of a realistic utopia.

If you think an existing, crucial behavior or value is threatened by a general world trend—this is an opportunity for preservation. Use these negative movements from what *was* to what *might be* to inform your utopian vision.

Remember—the essentials of a perfect world that move you most, intellectually *and* emotionally, are all that matter when determining the meaning of your life, *not* what you think others will deem most important, politically correct, or cool.

Write your statements beginning with something such as *In a perfect world...* or *In my utopia...*

1.

2.

3.

4.

5.

6.

7.

8.

CONGRATULATIONS. You have built your Ideals Code.

DETERMINING THE MEANING OF
YOUR LIFE

What Moves You

Now you have a short list of important behaviors, values, and issues that conflict with or conform to your own (but are at risk), written in the form of an Ideals Code.

In most cases, by this point, you probably have a good idea of what moves you and what you deeply care about. If none of your answers move you intellectually and emotionally (meaning you become emotional when you think of it, get a little misty, or, if you are a he-man who does not cry, you're pretty sure you're having tear duct issues), that often means you're letting external forces influence your answers. If this is the case, I suggest you clear your mind, revisit the previous chapters and questions, and conduct some honest internal dialogue. The meaning of life needs to be the meaning of *your* life, not someone else's.

It's crucial to make certain the thing that draws you to it, or the conflict you most want to fight for or against, is not your choice because you think it *should* be or because it's what you're expected to care the most about.

This decision is the source from which your other decisions will flow. It's the meaning of your life, so analyze what you think and how you feel about the various value and behavior conflicts. Though the meaning of your life will likely be a statement referring to something outside yourself, don't let external influences sway your judgment. This meaning will fuel your every step, so it must be yours. Deciding you need to join Greenpeace because the hot girl you're crushing on in the marketing department has a whale tattoo is flawed reasoning.

Assuming for now one of the items on your Ideals Code moves you, let's look at that one. Place it into something resembling the following statement:

"My Moral Code, *Values Code, Ideals Code, reason, experience, and passion lead me to think (insert the meaning of your life) is the (biggest threat to the world/best thing about the world that is at risk/most pressing problem in the world)."*

Here are some examples:

"My Moral Code, *Values Code, Ideals Code, reason, experience, and passion lead me to think the lack of clean drinking water in underdeveloped countries is the most pressing problem in the world."*

"My Moral Code, *Values Code, Ideals Code, reason, experience, and passion lead me to think the lack of access to quality healthcare is the biggest threat to my country."*

"My Moral Code, *Values Code, Ideals Code, reason, experience, and passion lead me to think religious radicalism is the biggest threat to the world."*

"MY MORAL CODE, *Values Code, Ideals Code, reason, experience, and passion lead me to think affordable college education is the best thing about my country that is at risk."*

NOW WRITE YOUR STATEMENT:

"My Moral Code, Values Code, Ideals Code, reason, experience, and passion lead me to think..."

NOW THAT YOU'VE written down what could be the meaning of your life, how does it look? Is it important enough to you? Does it mean enough to you? Can it fuel your life?

Once you're satisfied you know the meaning of your life, it's time to take the next step and turn meaning into purpose.

PART
THREE

PART THREE
THE PURPOSE OF LIFE

Purpose is how you act upon your meaning. It means you fight for something or fight against something. It is determined by translating the meaning of your life into action.

TRANSLATING MEANING INTO PURPOSE

A Matter of Scale

Meaning and purpose are sometimes used interchangeably, but not here. Purpose is an action that reinforces or fights for a meaning that exists in the world in a positive state *or* that provides a solution to or fights against a meaning that exists in a negative state.

Like defining the meaning of your life, determining your purpose is necessarily an internal process. Searching *externally* for purpose will sever the internal connection you've built between yourself and the meaning of your life. It will continue the disconnect you've sensed all your life, reinforce the constraints of *don't*, and hamstring all that you would *do*. Perhaps most damaging, searching externally for purpose allows others to determine the course of your life.

Internally searching for purpose connects *your* action to *your* thoughts and unique worldview. A happy consequence is that searching internally for purpose prevents a homogenization of purpose across humanity. There are a lot of things in this great big world that need a champion, and avoiding the issues du jour and the barrage of *you should be a...* will not only bring you deeper fulfillment but might also make the world a better place.

Often, purpose is a big thing, addressing something important in the world (your meaning) on many levels. However, it can also be a big issue acted upon on a small scale (such as combating a perceived lack of educational quality in the world by teaching your children how to think rationally and critically).

Irrespective of scale, just as the meaning of your life must move you both intellectually and emotionally, it's crucial your purpose inspires you, because how much it excites you will determine your day-to-day level of fulfillment.

Meaning runs deep. Purpose aims high.

An inspiring, challenging purpose, derived from a moving meaning, makes action easy, whereas an uninspiring purpose results in a life of drudgery.

Sometimes knowing where to begin is the key bit of knowledge. Do you start small? Do you need big goals? The scale of your purpose should reflect your meaning and who you are or want to be. There's great power in the concept of taking a shower before you sweep up your house, sweeping up your house before you clean up the neighborhood, cleaning up the neighborhood before you rebuild the city, and so on. That said, if you're a world changer or a world saver, make the world your stage. As with all aspects of this book, you and the meaning of your life dictate the scale of your purpose.

Purpose Questions

As with the Moral Code, Values Code, and Ideals Code sections, if you need more room to write, do not wish to write in your book, or own the e-book or audiobook, download the PDF at tewhitaker.com.

WRITE the meaning of your life here:

Now BEGIN TRANSLATING the meaning of your life into your life's purpose. Brainstorm for actions—paid or unpaid, free or costly—that would fight for or against the meaning of your life, depending on its positive or negative nature. At this stage, everything is on the table.

OF THE ACTIONS that would promote or combat the meaning of your life, which inspires you most and/or would be most effective?

Purpose Flowchart

The answer to the last question above is your interim purpose. The accompanying flowchart is a step-by-step process to determine whether your interim purpose is your true purpose. Begin in the top-left corner with your interim purpose. If you own the audiobook, download the flowchart PDF at tewhitaker.com.

START HERE

Is your interim purpose what you currently do for money?

YES → Do you want to remain with your current job or career, or do you want to do something else?

REMAIN → Can you shift or amplify the focus (if necessary) of what you currently do, or use part of your income and/or free time, to effectively fight for or fight against the meaning of your life?

SOMETHING ELSE

NO ↓

What job/process/activity have you always wanted to do?

Congratulations. You have determined your purpose.

YES ← Does it inspire you?

YES ↓   **NO** ↓

YES ← (from Can you shift...)

Does it inspire you? → **NO** (from current job)

See Notes below (#2).

NO ↓

Does your "dream job" effectively fight for or fight against the meaning of your life?

YES → Does it inspire you? → **NO** →

YES ↑

If you are unable to revise your current job or "dream job" to effectively fight for or fight against the meaning of your life, *and* inspire you, see #2 in the Notes below. If you still don't see a path forward, review the other potential actions from the brainstorming step, beginning with what inspires you the most, and analyze them with this flowchart until you have determined your purpose.

NO ↓

Could it be revised to effectively fight for or fight against the meaning of your life?

YES → How could it be revised?

NO ↓

If you are unable to revise it to effectively fight for or fight against the meaning of your life, see #2 in the Notes below. If you still don't see a path forward, review the other potential actions from the brainstorming step, beginning with what inspires you the most, and analyze them with this flowchart until you have determined your purpose.

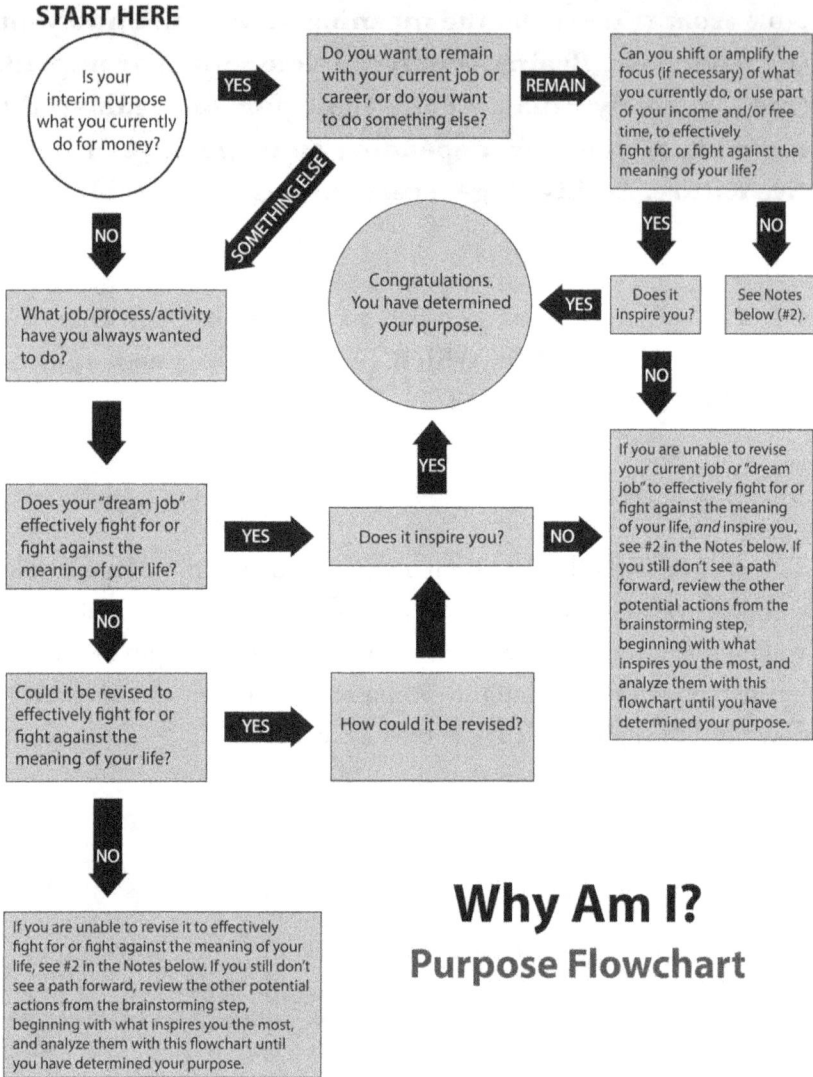

Why Am I?
Purpose Flowchart

Notes:
1) Do not leave this section until you've determined the purpose that inspires you and (if necessary) could support your needs.
2) Remember, though it is preferable for your purpose to support you financially (because we all have to live in this world, which requires money in exchange for goods and services), the reality of life is that most people perform their jobs and pursue their purposes concurrently. Don't unnecessarily delay pursuing your purpose because your established career and passion don't align. You *can* do both.

Final Thoughts on Purpose

Determining and acknowledging your life's purpose can be an excit-ing, frightening moment. The path from here to there teems with obstacles, gatekeepers, and fears both real and imagined. There will be hesitation and doubt. There will be inertia. There will be dragons.

Most people later say the happiest times of their lives were those when they were most challenged. Though there are thousands of books about making life a permanent vacation, it seems we were built for challenge, not leisure. Apparently, the ideal vacation is climbing a mountain.

Nothing worth anything is easy. If your purpose is something you haven't considered and prepared for your entire life, you'll have to take steps to *pursue* your purpose.

Write a statement in a form something like: "My Moral Code, Values Code, Ideals Code, reason, experience, and passion lead me to *think this about life* (meaning). Therefore, I am going to fight *for or against* it by *doing this* (purpose)."

Here are two different perspectives on purpose. The first is by someone who has a career he loves but an unrelated purpose. The second is from someone less committed to her current position.

- *My Moral Code, Values Code, Ideals Code, reason, experience, and passion lead me to think the lack of clean drinking water in underdeveloped countries is the most pressing problem in the world. Therefore, I am going to fight against it by setting aside fifty dollars from each paycheck to purchase a gravity-powered water filtration device and spend my annual vacation in the Sudan, delivering twenty-four water filtration devices to needy people, with help from a local NGO.*
- *My Moral Code, Values Code, Ideals Code, reason, experience, and passion lead me to think affordable college*

*education is the best thing about my country that is at risk.
Therefore, I am going to fight for it by developing an
online, accredited university that, for a nominal fee,
teaches and certifies people in new economy careers such
as computer science, sponsored by companies that need
employees with the specific skills my online university
teaches.*

Now craft your statement of purpose:

"My Moral Code, Values Code, Ideals Code, reason, experience, and passion lead me to think ..."

LIVING THE LIFE

Be More

ONE OF THE most important realizations you can have is that you want to be more—more than you are now, more than you've asked of yourself to this point, more than your friends or family expect or ask or think of you, more than anyone knows is inside you. The desire to be more is an internal drive, not a drive to equal or exceed an external standard. It doesn't mean you're isolated. It means you have more to give, more to contribute, more to be.

Living the life is about being more. If you're frustrated with your place in the world or the world in general, that can be a starting point. Why are you frustrated? What frustrates you? Questions such as these add depth to your life's meaning and purpose so long as your discoveries and subsequent actions aren't based on external influences such as jealousy.

A feeling of disenchantment with your place in the world, or a disconnect with the world at large, is a sign you want to be more, you want the world to be more, and you want more and better for everyone. Despite the many negative symptoms of our accumulation-oriented, politically polarized culture, there is a positive, growing aspect to it: Individuals want to be more and to contribute meaningfully to society as a whole.

Our society is structured for you to contribute in small ways to the economy and to the species while maintaining stability via employment and the institution of marriage. However, marriage and employment are often not enough to fulfill someone from an internal standard or to advance society in a meaningful way. They only maintain the status quo. George Bernard Shaw said:

> *The reasonable man adapts himself to the world; the unreasonable one persists in trying to adapt the world to himself. Therefore all progress depends on the unreasonable man.*

I'm not certain whether Shaw would have considered the goals of this book reasonable or unreasonable (maybe somewhere between). By determining your meaning and purpose, you are, in one way, basing your life on the reality of the world in which you live. On the other hand, you are rejecting external forces and agreed-upon meanings. By determining your life's meaning and purpose, you are adapting *your world* to yourself. Your world is immediately around you, the universe where you are the sun around which all else orbits.

That world is where you'll make progress. That world is where you'll first take your stand.

Is this unreasonable? I don't think so, though it's not maintaining the status quo. It echoes Ayn Rand's *Atlas Shrugged*, but instead of being a "producer," withdrawing yourself from the "moochers" and setting up a parallel civilization, you are an individual—withdrawing yourself from a well-worn, socially crafted life path and the culturally defined goals it upholds—cutting *your* path with *your* standards. Determining your life's meaning and purpose is far from unreasonable. If anything, it's the most reasonable, rational action you can take. By defining your life's meaning and purpose, you shape your reality instead of trying to fit the square *you* into the great round world.

A MORE YOU

The Key

OFTEN, if not always, you'll need to take steps to put yourself in a position to pursue your purpose and to get from where and who you are now to where and who you want to be. There will be skills to learn, education to obtain, and moves to make.

You can be who you want to be and do anything you want to do as long as you're willing to start from where you are right now. Too often the audacity of an action, the seemingly insurmountable path necessary to get from here to there, or resistance from those closest to us, stops us before we've started.

That won't be you. Not now.

Now that you've determined your life's meaning and purpose, you're likely feeling an energy flowing through you, a deep sense of certainty, and an anxiousness to get started. And maybe a little fear. Although pursuing your purpose is more akin to a marathon, it helps to start with a sprint.

The necessary steps you take, whether they include formal

education or informal erudition, should be looked upon as "bang-for-the-buck" experiences. By beginning *and* completing the preparation phase as quickly as you can, whether that means months or years, you establish momentum.

There are a few questions to ask yourself. As before, if you prefer not to write in this book or you have the e-book or audiobook, download the questions and purpose flowchart PDF at tewhitaker.com.

WHAT SKILLS ARE necessary for you to pursue your life's purpose?

WILL YOU NEED FORMAL EDUCATION, or is it possible to attain the knowledge you need through erudition (self-taught)? Will you need a traditional degree to execute your purpose or to legitimize your voice? Often erudition can take the place of formal education except in cases where professional degrees (or letters such as PhD behind your name) legitimize you as an expert.

HOW LONG WILL it take to attain the skills necessary to promote or combat your meaning?

WHAT IS the first step you can take toward developing your skills or obtaining the education you need to pursue your purpose?

Speed of Implementation

Take a close look at the first step toward pursuing your purpose. Don't wait until you finish this book. Do it today. It's important to take immediate action toward pursuing your purpose, no matter how small the step. One of the most important aspects of accomplishing anything is taking action *now*—to establish momentum and solidify commitment.

Maybe best of all, by taking immediate steps toward living the life, you're already living with purpose. Remember that living with purpose is rewarded with fulfillment. This is the beauty of knowing the meaning behind what you're doing. Understanding what drives you opens up possibilities you may not have considered, clarifies the decision-making process, and transforms fulfillment from an occasional feeling of achievement into a day-to-day experience.

Momentum

Momentum does not just happen. Momentum is built by your actions. By acting immediately, and taking steps every day toward the training and/or education necessary to pursue your purpose, you build momentum to push through the inevitable obstacles, disappointments, and difficulties that face anyone striving to be more.

Keep in mind there is *always* something you can do to move yourself forward, to make an impact, and to maintain momentum even if you're waiting for notification, acceptance, or the beginning of formal training. Determining your life's meaning and purpose are the important first steps of living the life, but you still have to possess the courage and determination to actually *do it*.

That said, if you've nailed the meaning of your life, it's likely you're more inspired and motivated than you've ever been, so devouring more information related to your meaning and finding new avenues to pursue your life's purpose might seem effortless.

Embodiment

There are many well-worn phrases illustrating the idea of embodiment such as "dress for the job you want, not the job you have." This is another excellent aspect of understanding what moves you and why. You are internally "dressing" for who you're going to be while gathering the knowledge, background, and education necessary to pursue your life's purpose and meaning. Because of this, you'll experience fulfillment while preparing.

But the idea of "dressing" doesn't hit the mark of what you'll experience. The difference between dressing for success and embodying who you're going to be—based on your understanding of your life's meaning—is stark. It is as different as an actor portraying a real-life character and the walking, talking, real-life person being portrayed. A better perspective is that you are, for the first time, shedding the costume you've worn your entire life, the uniform you were loaned at birth and expected to wear until death. By developing your codes and your life's meaning and purpose, you've dug through the false layers to who you *really* are. You, meet you.

A clear understanding of what moves you intellectually and emotionally transforms life's usual assortment of dilemmas and false steps into easier choices and decisive moves, each based on how it serves the pursuit of your purpose. Embodying your life's meaning from the first step simplifies decisions. The uncertain grays of life sharpen to black and white.

In practice, embodiment is but a brief phase in your process, continuing only as long as it takes for you to redefine yourself.

Redefining Yourself

Sometimes becoming who you want to be necessitates redefining yourself to yourself, your friends, and your family. It can be challenging.

Years ago, I decided I would be a vegetarian. I made my (admittedly) holier-than-thou pronouncement a few days before Thanksgiving. It was met with civil yet open hostility and a few responses of "don't think we're cooking anything special for you" from the PTC (Pro-Turkey Crowd).

I spent the holiday eating dinner rolls, carrots, pumpkin pie, and enough sunflower seeds to fill a Yankee Stadium dugout. For twelve years, I continued with vegetarianism (pescatarianism without the shellfish component, to be exact), and my family, in general, never accepted it. When I decided to eat beef again, I was welcomed back to the fold with open arms.

This brief on my pescatarian past is to illustrate that redefining yourself is rarely comfortable when it comes to friends and family, because they see you in a certain way. Forcing them to see you in a new way is challenging. Change can be difficult. You can affect your own change, but you cannot change others or how they view you. The best you can do is to be an example.

When it comes down to it, no one really cares what you do with your life. Your parents, friends, or children will adjust to the new you, but they're generally worried about the basics. Will you starve? Will you be out on the streets? Will they be forced to take you in? Usually, friends and family are more concerned about whether your new purpose will impact *them* negatively than whether it will impact *you* positively.

That's why, in retrospect and with the benefit of hindsight, I highly recommend *against* pronouncing anything even if you're like me and have a taste for drama. Avoid the press conference and get on with it. Instead of shock and awe, go ninja. By the time anyone close to you realizes you've changed, you will already be a positive example of how to live.

Fear Transcendence

Fear often reveals itself as comfort, laziness, or procrastination, and it gets in the way of being more than you are now. The steps necessary to live the life you want to live seem too hard or boring. Maybe it's unnecessary. Maybe the way things are now is how it's supposed to be.

There are so many things to be afraid of when it comes to achieving a dream that it often feels safer to leave it as a dream and talk about it rather than pursue it. Maybe I should have kept my frustrations to myself, not spoken to my brother about them, assumed I knew better than anyone else, and remained a coffee shop philosopher instead of putting what I thought on these pages.

Maybe it would have been easier to keep quiet and play my role. Maybe it would have been safer to not risk rejection or being ignored.

Easier and safer, maybe. But not better.

Looking back, I've probably lived a good chunk of my life in fear of being wrong or misunderstood or offending the beliefs or ideals of others.

There is also a feeling—particularly when you've completed college, are an established professional, have a good (or safe) job, and have children—that it's too late, life has already dealt your cards, you're too old. Every one of these applies to me. How many apply to you?

The first truth is there's always a way to live your purpose that won't negatively impact your family. You can go back to college if that's what it takes to pursue the purpose of your life. Are you established in your industry? People change careers all the time—why not you? If you just can't do it, there are countless ways to fight for or against any meaning of life without quitting your job.

The second truth is that once you transcend the fear and start preparations to live the life, you're already fulfilling your life's purpose, and your days—good and bad—will possess meaning you've never known before. The smallest steps bloat with meaning, and there is a feeling of importance to almost everything you do.

It is never too late to make a difference for yourself or in the lives of others. Life never stops dealing cards. If you are reading this, you are not too old. It's not too late. It is never too late.

There is no better time to pursue your life's purpose, no era with less to lose, no more crucial moment to define your life's standards, the qualities of your fulfillment, your morals and values and ideals. We are, all of us, expendable to the monsters of indifference and excess. We are not, any of us, beholden to anyone or any things. We must, each of us, define our meaning, our purpose, our moment.

An Expanded Statement of Purpose

Expand your statement of purpose to include the steps necessary to pursue the purpose of your life. It might read something like these examples:

- *My Moral Code, Values Code, Ideals Code, reason, experience, and passion lead me to think the lack of clean drinking water in underdeveloped countries is the world's most pressing problem. Therefore, I am going to fight against it by setting aside fifty dollars from each paycheck to purchase a gravity-powered water filtration device and spend my annual vacation in the Sudan, delivering twenty-four water filtration devices to needy people, with help from a local NGO. To do this, I need to find the best filtration device and the most effective Sudan-based NGO, and set up my online banking to automatically transfer fifty dollars to a new account.*
- *My Moral Code, Values Code, Ideals Code, reason, experience, and passion lead me to think affordable college education is the best thing about my country that is at risk. Therefore, I am going to fight for it by developing an online, accredited university that, for a nominal fee, teaches and certifies people in new economy careers such as computer science, sponsored by companies that need employees with the specific skills my online university teaches. To accomplish this, I need to learn computer*

science, determine which coding languages and careers are the most useful and needed, build a website, and approach companies as potential hiring partners.

Now craft your expanded statement of purpose:
"My Moral Code, Values Code, Ideals Code, reason, experience, and passion lead me to think ..."

PART
FOUR

PART FOUR
FULFILLMENT

Fulfillment is not a prize or a victory. It shouldn't come only at the end of life, after reaching a goal, or when you buy something shiny. Fulfillment is something you should experience every day. This is possible only by detaching fulfillment from the achievement and connecting it to the endeavor. The endeavor is the thing. If you pursue your life's meaning and purpose every day, you'll experience fulfillment every day. Fulfillment is intellectual and emotional immersion in meaningful and purposeful action.

A CONSTANT FEELING

Peak Experience

IN MOST BELIEF SYSTEMS, fulfillment is what you get at the end, maybe after a purchase or after your death. For those looking to sell you a car or a phone, positioning fulfillment as a repeatable process is intelligent and lucrative. You get a little dose of fulfillment with every two-year wireless contract and every forty-two-month car lease. For those looking to sell the impossible-to-prove-or-disprove victory over death, its impossible-to-prove-or-disprove-ness is smart and profitable.

Fulfillment should be—and is—an all-encompassing, consciousness-filling acknowledgment. It is, by definition, an internal experience. You *experience* it. You are not *given* it. You do not *buy* it. Somewhere along the way, we've allowed those with something to sell to define fulfillment as an external experience to be bought or rewarded. Either you're fulfilled in short bursts during life, or you get it after death.

There is a better way. By pursuing your life's meaning and purpose, you'll experience fulfillment on a daily basis—a consistent feeling of direction, purpose, and meaning. You'll experience an attainable and knowable reward *while you are alive* without the judgment of an outside authority. Fulfillment is a real (in the "not fake" sense of the word) alternative to externally promoted goals such as heaven, paradise, Valhalla, becoming one with the material universe, peer recognition, job promotions, celebrity, fame, infamy.

By defining fulfillment as the internal experience of an ongoing, meaningful action instead of material attainment or a destination-based goal, fulfillment becomes a steady state of being, a constant recognition that your every action contributes to what's most important to you.

Fulfillment is a lifelong, ongoing, personal quality-of-life index, determined by the extent to which you live within the framework of pursuing your life's meaning and purpose.

Flow

In his book, *Flow: The Psychology of Optimal Experience*, Mihaly Csikszentmihalyi proposed that people experience a state of "flow" when they are in a state of concentration or complete absorption with the activity at hand and the situation. According to Csikszentmihalyi's research, people often cite (in retrospect) the most difficult challenges they've faced as the best times of their lives. Entrepreneurs often say they loved their work more while building their company than after the business succeeded. The best athletes work tirelessly on nameless fields with no cameras because they *love* it, because they are in flow. It's the obsession with a challenge, the total immersion in a daunting task, that gives us the sensation of time flying, of accomplishment, of *flow*.

George Mallory—an English mountaineer who died on the north face of Mount Everest in 1924—was asked, after having failed twice to reach Everest's summit, why he wanted to climb the world's highest peak.

"Because it's there," he said.

I suspect Mallory's famous response came from a place much

deeper in him than its nonchalance suggests. I think his quote survived through the years because we all understand what he really meant. *There*, on the mountain face, suspended above certain death and below a difficult goal, was where he felt alive. Mallory experienced flow when climbing mountains.

How does flow relate to pursuing the purpose of your life? It's a barometer of sorts. The feeling of flow described by Csikszentmihalyi is the feeling of fulfillment for which we all strive. Experiencing a continuous sense of flow is the goal, the grail, the grand prize.

Using the process outlined in this book, you should now have a clear purpose in life, a sense of how you're going to pursue your purpose, and a mix of surging excitement and uncertainty. With a clear, inspiring purpose, developed from the meaning of your life, you will experience flow *while* you pursue your purpose and while you develop any new skills necessary to pursue it. In other words, you will experience fulfillment the moment you begin to pursue your purpose.

The pursuit of purpose is what life is all about. A primary aspect of life is challenge. By choosing the challenges you face each day and defining their meaning, you deepen your potential for immersion in the actions you take. You build a platform for flow, for fulfillment.

For fulfillment to occur, there must be challenge. If your goal is constant fulfillment, the actions involved in pursuing your purpose must be challenging. A learning, striving, reaching life is a fulfilling life. A purpose that doesn't present ongoing challenges won't reward you with continuing fulfillment.

There are probably many things at which you're good, but that doesn't mean they will—or should—all contribute to your life's purpose. Often, what we're good at is simply what's easy for us. This diminishes the challenge aspect of flow unless you're *always* trying to get better at something or if, like Mallory, what you're good at is intensely difficult. If you eliminate the challenge from pursuing your purpose, you'll have a tough time realizing fulfillment.

That said, if you capitalize on what you're good at by using it to directly fight for or against your meaning—*while* challenging yourself —that *is* one way to live a fulfilling life. There is almost *always* a way to challenge yourself, even with something you've done for years. Challenging action, to support a purpose driven by the meaning of your life, results in fulfillment.

By infusing your "every breath" (pardon the melodrama) with meaning, and challenging yourself with how you pursue your purpose, you'll find a consistent state of fulfillment.

THE YOU EVOLUTION

Life as a Loop

EVERYTHING to this point has led to you. This life is the moment, *your* moment. Birth is the beginning of your moment, and death is the end. Between the existential bookends are your clock ticks. Arguments for the time before birth and an eternity after death are moot. Life—our consciousness, the reality we see and feel and experience and consider—is the only reality we know. All other stages, spaces, dimensions, destinations, and beliefs are speculation, fantasy, arguable, and unknowable. Basing your life on what you *know*—not what you *believe*—is the only way to live in this world's reality.

The same goes for experiencing fulfillment.

By defining your fulfillment as an internal standard, a feeling unassociated with external approval, attached to the verifiable reality you experience every day, life becomes a self-contained, positively charged, infinite loop of meaning, purpose, living, and fulfillment. You can analyze for relevance anything you do or consider—with the meaning and purpose of your life as the guiding factors. You now base important questions and answers on *your* life as opposed to someone else's life and standards—celebrities, friends, or self-proclaimed social media superstars.

"What will I do?"

"How will this affect the pursuit of my purpose?"

"Am I deriving fulfillment from what I'm doing?"

Life-affecting decisions now have a framework. The framework you create provides a productively navigable context in which to live.

"Does this contribute or detract from my life's purpose?"

"If I do this, will I feel more or less fulfilled?"

By positioning your fulfillment as a continuing measurement, your life's meaning and purpose can stay the same or evolve, depending on new experiences and decisions. If the meaning and purpose of your life evolves, the meaning-purpose-living-fulfillment loop self-adjusts, with fulfillment continuing as your internal barometer.

If you feel your sense of fulfillment flagging, there's a good chance you should revisit your meaning. There are some people who, at nine or twelve or sixteen years old, know the meaning of their lives and base their lives upon their heightened self-knowledge. Most of us are not so self-reflective, and external sources have compromised us by the time we get around to determining the meaning of life (if we ever do). As we grow older and gather experiences, as wisdom takes root, new thoughts and beliefs emerge. The evolution of the meaning of your life is natural and important to recognize if you want to experience lifelong fulfillment.

Go through the questions again if you feel your sense of fulfillment diminishing. By revisiting (and maybe revising) your Moral Code, Values Code, and Ideals Code, and evaluating the conclusions that result from the interaction of those codes, you can determine how you've changed and, if necessary, redefine the meaning of your life.

If you redefine your meaning, you'll likely want to adjust your purpose and how you pursue it. Like everything else, you naturally change as time passes. It isn't a scary thing. The change within you signals maturity and evolution.

Recognizing these changes enables slight nudges along the way to stay the course, eliminating existential crises and depression.

O Captain, My Captain

By experiencing fulfillment every day, your life becomes the self-determined realization of all the promises made by the religions, prophets, and gurus, your parents and high school guidance counselor, Silicon Valley, Wall Street, Madison Avenue, and Hollywood. By deriving the meaning of your life, you are no longer held to the mythical, self-denial-driven standards of ancient or medieval minds, or the messages of material gluttony we hear throughout our days. Rather, your fulfillment is a product of your decisions, values, ideas, and morals. Your happiness is based on your time, experiences, and evaluations.

By whose standard? Yours. Who decides? You do.

You've lived long enough to know you know yourself better than anyone else and that allowing others to navigate your life for you will leave you on the rocks, dissatisfied.

By knowing the meaning and purpose of your life and pursuing that purpose, you retake the wheel and are bound for fulfillment.

You are the captain of your ship.

CONCLUSION

Scaling Significance

RECENTLY I'VE WATCHED several speakers finish their talks with the famous "pale blue dot" photo of Earth—shot by Voyager I from a distance of 3.7 billion miles—along with one portion or another of astronomer Carl Sagan's equally famous quote (from his book *Pale Blue Dot: A Vision of the Human Future in Space*) to draw our attention to the insignificance of human folly in the sheer vastness of things.

This perspective holds if we're considering all of humanity or the entirety of space, but significance versus insignificance is a matter of scale.

Am I significant in relation to the universe's wondrous spread? No. It's too vast, and what's beyond the black is unknown, maybe unknowable.

Will anything you do have any consequence whatsoever on the inevitable demise of our planet? No. Eventually, inexorably, the sun's heavier elements will fuse, our favorite star will expand to red giant size and envelop or incinerate our planet, and nothing—fame or infamy, wealth or poverty, wonderful deeds or terrible—will make the slightest difference.

Can we cause change—good or bad—in our world? Maybe. Consider the genius of Einstein, Mozart, and da Vinci. The atrocities of Hitler and Stalin. Harriet Tubman's courage. Amelia Earhart.

Can you contribute to those around you? Yes. You can embody meaning and purpose for your children. You can be a good friend. You can lead by example. You can positively influence others by living a meaningful life.

Can you make a difference in your life? Definitely. Our significance and power reside within us, and from there they emanate, rolling out like ripples on a pond.

Each of us is the most significant entity to ourselves. Our actions are the only actions over which we have direct control. Accordingly, most of us go through life believing we are our own masters, while a single hard glance proves us flotsam upon waves of media hype, materialism, and fleeting trends, lashed to this god or that, swayed by others' opinions, numbed by routine.

You can change all that.

Determine the meaning of your life. Translate it into purpose. Live the life. Experience fulfillment every day.

It can be a steep climb from who you are now to who you want to be. Before you've established momentum, simple-to-scale obstacles will seem insurmountable peaks. Your challenge's sheer audacity and the height to which you're aiming might prompt the question, "Why am I even doing this?"

Because you're here.

THANKS FOR READING

Did you enjoy reading *Why Am I?* If so, please leave a review and let me and other readers know. Thank you!

ALSO BY TODD WHITAKER

Why Am I? Find the Meaning of Life, Live with Purpose, Succeed on Your Terms

Writing as T. E. Whitaker

Into Temptation

Chronicles of Vajra series

LA LA Land

Crazy Eyes

The Rooster Rides

ABOUT THE AUTHOR

TODD WHITAKER is an author, filmmaker, and philosopher. Raised in Iowa across the road from a corn field, he moved to Southern California after graduating from the University of Iowa, and now drinks espresso and writes at a café table in Las Vegas. He is the author of *Into Temptation*, the *Chronicles of Vajra* series, and *Why Am I?* You can sign up for his newsletter at tewhitaker.com.

CONNECT

tewhitaker.com
todd@tewhitaker.com

facebook.com/tewhitakerofficial

twitter.com/TE_Whitaker

instagram.com/t.e.whitaker

www.ingramcontent.com/pod-product-compliance
Lightning Source LLC
LaVergne TN
LVHW051132080426
835510LV00018B/2365